Paternalistic Capitalism

Paternalistic Capitalism

Andreas G. Papandreou

THE UNIVERSITY OF MINNESOTA PRESS

MINNEAPOLIS

HB
87
P26
1972

Library of Congress Catalog Card Number: 79-187169

ISBN 0-8166-0631-5

The quotation on pages 37 to 39 from
E. J. Mishan, The Costs of Economic Growth, is
reprinted by permission of Granada Publishing
Limited, London, and Praeger Publishers, Inc.,
New York. The quotation on pages 111 to
114 is from The Power Elite by C. Wright Mills.
Copyright © 1956 by Oxford University Press,
Inc. Reprinted by permission.

*To my children,
George, Sophia, Nicholas
and Andreas, with the wish
that they contribute to
the building of a rational
social order*

Preface

The basic themes of *Paternalistic Capitalism* evolved over a
number of years as a result of an increasingly intense realization that my conceptual apparatus—as an economist—was
woefully inadequate for giving me even a reasonable understanding of the realities of the power structure that dominate
life in the contemporary society of the West.

Generations of mainline or orthodox economists have been
successful in erecting a truly imposing logical framework for
a unified explanation of economic phenomena. Yet, as the
unity, the logical precision, and the elegance of the conceptual
edifice were perfected, its inadequacies as an explanatory
scheme for the essentially evolutionary and power-dominated
social processes of the world we live in became glaringly evident. This understanding is no longer limited to a small circle
of apprehensive professional economists. It is shared increasingly by the new generation of economists and by a widening
circle of policy-oriented professionals in the West, as well as
by the intellectual communities that play a leading role in
shaping the societies of the developing countries.

In *Paternalistic Capitalism* I have done more than just give
vent to these apprehensions. I have attempted, in fact, to
sketch a rough outline of the basic economic, social, and politi-

cal dynamic of contemporary capitalism, especially as it displays itself in the Western metropolis, the United States of America.

Even a casual glance at the book will suggest that the interpretation I offer differs radically from the orthodox, conventional interpretation. My interpretation, though radical, does not fit a dogmatic mold. For I am altogether too impressed by the limits of our understanding of contemporary society to allow myself the luxury of proposing a tightly worked-out alternative interpretive scheme. I have written the book in the hope that it will contribute to a serious debate which may further our understanding of modern capitalism, and facilitate our search for meaningful and socially acceptable alternatives.

I wish to express my appreciation to my colleagues and students at York University who knowingly or not have contributed much to the shaping of my thoughts. More particularly I want to thank my good friend Stanley Sheinbaum for urging me to engage in this venture and Richard Parker of Magdalen College, Oxford, for his valuable comments and suggestions.

My warm thanks go to Angela Kokkola, who struggled through the typing of the first version of this book, and to Christine Sloan, who typed the final version. I am grateful to Margaret Papandreou for her careful reading of the complete manuscript and for her many substantive and stylistic contributions to its final form.

Andreas G. Papandreou

November 28, 1971
King City, Ontario

viii

Contents

Paternalistic Capitalism

A Distortion
of Vision

The spectacular growth of the social sciences — and especially of economics — has tended to obscure and distort rather than elucidate our vision, our understanding of the processes of the social system of which we were destined to be a part. This distortion of our vision of contemporary society has many roots. One of them may well be traced to scientific inertia. Having developed in the past a set of tools and concepts possibly appropriate for the interpretation of the behavior and the evaluation of the performance of yesterday's society, we unwittingly continue to employ them in a social environment which has changed in profound ways. And this seems to be true not only of the orthodox or main-line interpretations, but to some extent of many of the radical critiques of the "system" as well. Another root may be traced to the arbitrary definition of the frontiers of the various social sciences. Each discipline — economics, sociology, political science, and so forth — has erected tenacious fences around the analytical and empirical territory it claims for itself. Strongly enforced professional standards identify successful careers with work in conventionally circumscribed problem areas. But social processes cannot always be effectively dissected or partitioned into the arbitrary categories that under-

3

lie the structure of the social sciences. Many important problems — possibly, the most important — fall between stools, in no-man's-land. But there is a third, dominant root of social myopia. Clear vision, and penetrating analysis of a social system, any social system, becomes almost unavoidably identified with radical critique, a medicine that no social system can tolerate, except in very small doses. The process of selection of the leaders, those who set the pace and the style of work in the social sciences, is splendidly adapted to the task of excluding, or relegating to the margin, those who engage in radical critique. Thus, with the exception of genuinely revolutionary periods, conventional and fundamentally uncritical ways of looking at society become entrenched; they become ideologies.

I shall argue in this book that the prevalent interpretation, analysis, and evaluation of contemporary capitalism is ideologically biased. I am not suggesting that the prevalent beliefs are not genuinely held. Quite to the contrary. They are genuinely and tenaciously held, for otherwise they would constitute a very poor ideology. Needless to say, in taking such a stand I run the danger of being accused of arrogance. To suggest that the main-line interpretation of contemporary capitalism is ideologically biased, and therefore myopic, may be taken to mean that I consider my own vision as being superior. I do not claim that. Rather, I shall outline a new interpretation, an interpretation quite different from the conventional one.

Although I have drawn heavily on radical critique and analysis, the book is more than a composite of or a selection from contemporary radical literature. It offers, I believe, a new synthesis and a new view of contemporary capitalism, especially American capitalism, both at home and abroad. I do not restrict myself to an economic interpretation, attempting to encompass as many aspects of the relevant social processes as my awareness and training permit. Naturally, there are many aspects of contemporary capitalist society that I have had to neglect, especially those related to cultural, sociological, and socio-psychological dimensions.

The strategy of the book is quite straightforward. The first chapter, "The Myth of Market Capitalism," is a critique of the accepted interpretation of the contemporary capitalist economy. I have tried to present my argument in a way that should permit the general reader to understand the orthodox view and to become sharply aware of its limitations and shortcomings; and I urge the nonprofessional reader not to skip this chapter because of its seemingly technical character. Basically, there are two themes running through the chapter. The first theme is that economists are guilty of extending to our own socio-economic environment conclusions drawn from an abstractly defined and sharply different environment. Thus, a myth has evolved and become entrenched concerning the alleged overall beneficence (efficiency and effectiveness) of the market mechanism in allocating scarce resources in contemporary capitalism — when in fact this beneficence can be shown to be a property only of a market economy that has little in common with contemporary capitalism. The second theme is that the capitalist economy of today is *not* in fact a market economy, at least not in the sense in which we normally use the term *market*.

But if it is not a market economy, if it is not market capitalism, then what is it? In "A Neo-Marxist View of the Capitalist Metropolis," I consider one possible interpretation — namely, the Neo-Marxist position, as presented by Baran and Sweezy, that contemporary capitalism can be best understood as monopoly capitalism. I find much of the Neo-Marxist argument valid, but discuss one truly major disagreement in the following chapter. The disagreement is simply this: The Neo-Marxists adopt the conventional view that the contemporary capitalist economy is basically a market economy. I do not — and this, indeed, is the central theme of the book. I should mention in passing that while presenting the Neo-Marxist argument, I attempt a useful reformulation of the concepts of surplus and social waste.

The third chapter, "Paternalistic Capitalism: The Economy," begins with a discussion of the technocratic interpretation of contemporary society presented by Galbraith in *The New Industrial State*. This interpretation contrasts sharply, despite many similarities, with the Neo-Marxist position. Galbraith's emphasis on "planning by the technostructure" motivates the key theme of the chapter: the formulation of the salient features of an economic model of paternalistic capitalism, a model that interprets the structure and behavior of the contemporary capitalist economy. Under this interpretation the market mechanism is on its way to becoming an instrument of privatized, decentralized planning by the corporate managerial elite. Sovereign is not the consumer but the corporate establishment, which participates in a super-game with the labor establishment and the state elite. Resources are allocated *through* the market, but not *by* the market. Thus, planning is a feature of contemporary capitalism, but it is *not* social planning. Rather, it is planning by the private managerial elite, in search of the highest practicable profits. Clearly, the term *paternalistic*, as used in this book, is entirely stripped of any implication that it may be benevolent (except, perhaps, from an autocrat's point of view). The privatized planning is not carried out in the interest of the consumer, but in the interest of the system; thus, *paternalistic* is intended to convey the autocratic, big brotherish aspect of the process.

The fourth chapter, "Paternalistic Capitalism: The State," is devoted to an exploration of the relationship between the managerial-capitalist elite and the instrumentalities that make up the state. In order to bring out this relationship against a proper historical and analytical background, I undertake a systematic examination of the meanings of and connections among the concepts of the state, the establishment, and the ruling class. The conclusions are not too surprising. The apex of the system of power over the society, the economy, the state in the prototype capitalist society, the society of the United States, is occupied by the corporate managerial-capitalist elite. But that elite does not stand alone. Next to it stands that component of the state elite which is responsible for the management of national security, the national security managers. Characteristically, they wear three-button suits, being members of the same social group from which the corporate managers are recruited. Other participants in the Establishment, though in a subservient role, are the hard hats (assimilated labor leaders) and the think tank experts (scientists who have placed themselves in the service of the system). Thus, the state in paternalistic capitalism serves the Establishment and through it the dominant and ruling class.

The presence of national security managers in a prominent position in the Establishment is no accident. For paternalistic capitalism is aggressively expansionist, and therefore imperialistic and militaristic. The fifth chapter, "Peaceful Coexistence and Counterrevolution," deals mainly with the foreign policy of the capitalist metropolis, the United States, in the evolving dialectic of peaceful coexistence with the socialist super-power, the Soviet Union. But even more basic, more lasting, is the counterrevolutionary motif which provides the dominant explanation for the assumption by the United States of the role of imperial peace-keeper.

The expansionist character of paternalistic capitalism is not primarily militaristic but, rather, a reflection of the laws of motion of the social system as a whole, which tends to reproduce everywhere on the geosphere the structure of social relations that support it at home. Therefore, the sixth chapter is devoted to the new mercantilism, the global aspect of paternalistic capitalism. The key institutional device for the system's expansion is the multinational corporation, which promotes the silent surrender of the hinterlands or peripheries of the expanding empire. Seen in this context, the Western concept of "development" of Third World countries is but a carefully designed path for their integration into an imperial structure of power. In contrast, the genuine quest for social and economic development, as expressed by the nationalist revolutionaries of the Third World, would carve out for the peripheries entirely different opportunities than would otherwise be available. And the quest calls, in general, for a confrontation with the metropolis-dominated Establishment. It identifies itself with national liberation, placing the political act ahead of the economic act.

Are there historically feasible alternatives to paternalistic capitalism? This is the central theme of the last, speculative chapter on social planning. Our attention is first drawn to the vast Soviet experiment. Is the Soviet type of socialism a desirable alternative to paternalistic capitalism? Even a cursory examination reveals that it, too, is paternalistic—that it is socialism only in the more or less perfunctory sense that productive wealth is owned and controlled by a state which, in turn, is controlled by a new class, the powerful party bureaucracy. The search for a type of society in which social planning —the conscious pursuit of articulated societal goals without domination by some establishment, be it of the bureaucratic or of any other type—can be realized leads to the concept of a regionally decentralized, socialist society. The vague outlines of a vision are drawn, the vision of a social order in which man will control rather than be at the mercy of his social environment.

The Myth of Market Capitalism

The faith of the common man in the West in the viability of the market economy was badly shaken from the experience of the thirties when a deep and persistent depression was highlighted by high unemployment and numerous business failures. It led to drastic reforms in the United States under the banner of Roosevelt's New Deal, and stoked the fires of fascism on the European continent. It is not possible to tell with certainty whether or not the New Deal would have restored full employment and buoyant business activity because the Second World War provided a full solution to all the depression-related problems that had bedeviled the nonfascist West. Actually, the problem was suddenly reversed: in the face of total mobilization in the war of "unconditional surrender," resource scarcity reasserted itself in an impressively sudden way.

Not surprisingly, the experience of the thirties came into sharp conflict with prevalent economic doctrine. According to orthodox tradition (what is now called the neoclassical model), involuntary unemployment of resources could only be the result of "frictions" and of "rigidities" or "stickiness" of their prices. Analytically, there was no room for an explanation of unemployment as a persistent or equilibrium feature of the market economy. Also not surprisingly, policies to combat unemployment erected on these foundations had a strong antilabor or antiunion flavor. For it was natural to argue that the downward stickiness of money wages—owing, according to the doctrine, to union practices—was the culprit.

This is the environment that gave birth to Keynes' revolution in economic thinking. What Keynes said, that there is nothing in the market economy which guarantees the full employment of resources, has become accepted doctrine. No economist is surprised any more by the fact that unemployment on a national scale persists despite the readiness of the unemployed to work at going wage rates. And only a handful of economists would argue that a fall in the wage rate would lead to the absorption of this type of unemployment.

The basic implications of the Keynesian analytical apparatus for a full-employment policy are quite simple: There exists a level of effective aggregate demand for an economy's aggregate product at full employment which just absorbs that product. The attainment of this level of effective aggregate demand cannot be left to the vagaries of the market. Thus, management of effective aggregate demand becomes a primary function of central government.

Keynesian analysis and policy does not challenge the foundations of orthodox doctrine and policy, for in no way does it question the basic role of the market mechanism in allocating resources to competing uses. The policy role assigned to central government, though important, is clearly auxiliary—not much more important than that, say, assigned to a thermostat set to maintain a constant temperature. The role of the government in Keynesian policy is essentially corrective.

In recent years economists' faith in the thermostatic role of central government has been shaken. To start with, we have become better acquainted with nationwide unemployment of resources which does not seem to respond to the standard treatment. The generation of higher levels of aggregate demand fails to absorb unemployment in depressed areas or in certain "excluded" groups, whether the exclusion of the group is based on age, education, color, language, or religion. This type of unemployment, which is not removable by Keynesian policy measures, has been called structural. The term *structural* suggests awareness that not all is well with the basic resource-allocating mechanism of the market economy.

A somewhat different problem with thermostatic, corrective policy-making has arisen as a result of the imposition of more complex target requirements on the central (government) control mechanism. If the policies are required to produce full employment, they may work well enough (as long as unemployment is not of a structural variety). However, if they are required to produce full employment *and* price stability, then the thermostat is strained to the breaking point. Not only is it increasingly harder to obtain full employment without inflation, but also, in the present large industrial economies of the West, a rather high rate of unemployment seems to go hand in hand with inflation. In this case, again, economists are forced to look to deeper, structural causes. In contrast with the depressed area or to the excluded group problem, this type of structural difficulty seems to involve the economic process in its totality. In fact, it seems to involve in a basic way the process of resource allocation in a market economy.

One need not stress the fact that there are other, pressing reasons for taking a hard new look at the market mechanism. The adverse side effects of industrial activities on the physical environment are a source of concern to governments and citizens alike. Somewhat more restricted, but no less vocal, is the concern over the quality of life produced for us by the "invisible hand of providence," the propelling-coordinating forces in the market economy. However, the task of taking a new look at the market mechanism of resource allocation is immensely difficult because the issue is deeply imbedded in an ideology[1] that has been put together over a period spanning two centuries. To begin with, it is strongly associated in the Western world with the concept of personal freedom, with distrust of central authority, and with democratic institutions, although in fact no one has established the necessary logical (as against merely historical) connections among these phenomena. This faith that a market economy is a necessary or a sufficient condition for a free society is itself a strong source of ideological bias.

But there is another, closely related source of such bias. How do we know the properties of the market mechanism? Clearly through the economist's analytical model of resource allocation in an abstractly defined market economy. Two questions arise immediately. First, are we entitled to extend our conclusions on the performance of the market mechanism, from some conveniently defined abstract environment to its performance in the environment of a contemporary capitalist economy? If not, what are the policy implications either for the role of the market or for capitalist institutions? Second, is the economist's model of the market economy adequate to the task of analysis of the behavior and evaluation of the performance of contemporary capitalism? That is to say, are we capable of understanding the essential characteristics of contemporary capitalism while holding onto the view that it is a market economy? This chapter is devoted to a cursory examination of the bias that springs from the manner in which economists deal with these issues.

*ECONOMIC EFFICIENCY

In an introductory book Robert Dorfman neatly sums up what impresses economists as being the signal contribution of

[1] An ideology is a systematic set of beliefs that justify and support a set of social institutions. The beliefs are *genuinely* held.

the market economy to social organization. "In spite of its intricacy, the basic idea of a free market economy is very simple. It is the idea of *decentralizing control* of the economy down to units of manageable proportions, coupled with a stupendously efficient method for conveying information among the decentralized units, and a highly effective method of motivating the units to perform their appropriate tasks efficiently."[2]

The truly central characteristic of a market economy is the information system which is identified with the parametric role of prices in a decentralized economic process. For any one unit (whether household or business firm) the prices of the commodities it buys or sells are beyond its control. They are given, universal bits of information for all the participants in the grand game. But though no unit is capable of affecting any of the prices through its purchases or sales, prices do respond to the independent, combined action of the multitude of participants in the markets. All prices are responsive to pressure: If aggregate demand for any commodity exceeds its aggregate supply in the market, the price is forced upward. The opposite is true when aggregate supply exceeds aggregate demand. The price of a commodity has no tendency to change, or is in equilibrium if aggregate demand for the commodity is just equal to its aggregate supply. Thus, equilibrium prices just clear the markets.

If this model is to be of interest as a piece of analytical apparatus, one must show that under certain conditions there exists a set of prices that equate aggregate supply to aggregate demand simultaneously in all markets. To state these conditions unambiguously, to establish that a general market equilibrium is theoretically possible, economists must spell out the

[2] *Prices and Markets* (Englewood Cliffs, N.J.: Prentice-Hall, 1967), p. 7. The emphasis is mine.

required features of the underlying or supporting social organization.[3] Specifically, they must state the manner in which information becomes available to the participants in the economic process; they must define in general terms the structure of authority or control; they must make some commitment as to the motivation of the participants; and, finally, they must describe the set of permissible moves (the legal framework) of the game. The specification of these conditions can be done in a fairly abstract manner and in alternative ways. In fact, the organizational requirements for a general market equilibrium have been spelled out for quite a few distinct models of market economies: for a crafts market economy, for the capitalist market economy, for a socialist market economy, for a labor-managed market economy, and so forth. In this book we restrict our attention to the capitalist model.

Not surprisingly, the model of the capitalist market economy, of market capitalism, was and is the central theme of economics in the West. Hence, taking a look at its principal features is worthwhile. To begin with, the role of the state is restricted to the task of providing the legal framework and ensuring that it is not violated. The basic features of the legal framework are private property and contract. Ownership or control of the economy's wealth is lodged in the hands of private persons. The government itself, of course, must own or control some property, if it is to perform its functions; but public ownership is commensurate to these functions, which are limited to the enactment and enforcement of the rules of the game.

The basic legitimate social process in such an economy is

[3] Actually, the model's analytical value depends also on whether or not general equilibrium has the property of being stable. If, when the system is shocked away from its equilibrium position, it has no tendency to return to it, then the properties of general equilibrium are of little interest. An economy that displays the features described here is called a *competitive* market economy. In this book the term *market economy* is intended to convey the same meaning.

exchange.[4] In fact, exchange is the dominant social process in all market economies because production of goods and services is not for one's own use but for the market. In market capitalism three conditions must be met in order that exchange take place. First, each of the parties to the exchange must own the commodity he intends to exchange. Second, he must be legally capable of transferring ownership to someone else. The law of property and contract establishes rules for identifying the owner of a commodity and the conditions under which a transfer may be carried out in a valid manner. Third, both parties must find it advantageous to complete the exchange. This is an essential feature of the total scheme, which is thus characterized as voluntaristic. In a well-developed market economy commodities are exchanged, not against other commodities, but against money. All commodities are for sale. The only complication worth mentioning affects the sale of labor. In a capitalist economy one may sell his labor time, but he may not sell himself; labor time is a commodity, but the owner of labor time is not. In a crafts market economy, composed exclusively of artisans or craftsmen, no one sells his labor time but only the product of his labor. In contrast, in a slave market economy, the workers themselves are bought and sold in the market.

In market capitalism, firms are controlled by an entrepreneur, who is either the owner or assumed to represent the owners of the net assets (assets minus liabilities) of the firm. The firm's task is conceived as the production of commodities through the (productive) consumption of other commodities. A firm engages, then, both in production and in exchange processes. Households are the ultimate owners of the productive services made available to the firms through the mar-

---

[4] In contrast to exchange, production is a technological process independent of the social context in which it takes place. Production takes place in every economy, whether it be feudal or tribal, capitalist or socialist. Exchange, on the other hand, is characteristic only of certain types of economies.

ket. They use the proceeds from the sale of these services to buy the commodities produced by the firms. Households, therefore, are both the ultimate sellers of productive services to the firms, and the ultimate buyers of the firm's products. Households, in contrast with firms, engage only in exchange processes.

Informationally, each firm is supposed to be familiar with its own technology and with the prices ruling in the market. Each household is supposed to be familiar with its own wants, tastes, or preferences; its own resources; and, of course, market prices. The system of prices may be viewed as the list of all the rates of transformation of commodities into money.

The scheme is completed by identifying the position or the state of rest of the participating units (households and firms) with an optimal state—that is, with a state in which some index (utility for the households, profit for the firms) is maximized subject to certain constraints. These indexes of well-being for the participating units incorporate a system of rewards motivating the units to perform their tasks efficiently.

It is worthwhile to take a more careful look at these indexes of well-being for the participating units. Given production technology and the prices of commodities, the entrepreneur is confronted with (infinitely) many feasible combinations of inputs and outputs of commodities. To each combination corresponds a profit (the difference between receipts and outlays). The model requires the firm to prefer more profits to less profits. Thus, the entrepreneur should select that combination which yields the maximum profit. Similarly for the household: given the prices of all commodities and the factors of production (productive services), the household is confronted with (infinitely) many feasible combinations of quantities of factors of production it might dispose of on the market with quantities of consumer goods it might acquire. To each such combination corresponds a level of satisfaction or utility, depending on the household's preferences or tastes. The model requires the household to prefer *more* to *less* utility. Thus, the household should select that combination of factor sales and consumer goods purchases which yields the maximum utility.

It follows, therefore, that in general equilibrium all markets are cleared, each household is in a position of maximum (feasible) utility, and each firm in a position of maximum (feasible) profits. Is it really surprising that, given this model, one can prove that competitive equilibrium (equilibrium in the kind of economy just described) is in some sense a socially optimal state of affairs? All one needs, in fact, is a nominalist view of society. Thus, we may agree that "society" is made "better off" if someone is made "better off" without somebody else being "worse off." And, in turn, a society could be said to be in an optimal position if no one can be made "better off" without somebody else being made "worse off." All this sounds terribly innocuous, but does have rather far-reaching implications, as we shall see later on in the argument.

We may ask, Who is to be the judge of whether some individual is "better off" or "worse off"? The natural (but not the only) extension of the model is to assume that he himself is to be the judge. This is the orthodox approach to the problem of social or economic welfare, identified with the Italian economist Vilfredo Pareto. Economists have proved that (under certain conditions) competitive equilibrium is Pareto-optimal (and vice versa). We must be careful in interpreting this proof. To begin with, it should be clear by the very meaning of the term *proof* that the Pareto-optimal character of competitive equilibrium is contained in its very definition. The equivalence between competitive equilibrium and Pareto-optimality is purely formal; the equivalence does not have the character of an empirical revelation. Second, it must be stressed that this type of social optimality refers *only* to efficiency, to the absence of waste in the economic process. Thus, when we say that a certain kind of equilibrium is Pareto-optimal, we mean that (given the resource-endowment of the economy, the prevalent technology, and the preferences of the individuals that make it up) no change is capable of making some individual "better off" without making some other individual "worse off." Thus, in fact, the key claim that can be made for this kind of economy is simply that it *eliminates waste in the allocation of resources.* To put it somewhat differently, resources are allocated according to the preferences of the households—which, in this sense, are sovereign—in an informationally economical fashion without any kind of central management or control.

The extension of this claim to the workings of some historically given market economy is legitimate only to the extent that the basic assumptions of the model are in fact satisfied historically. But before I turn to this question, I shall examine what the model has to say about the distribution of income and wealth.

* THE DISTRIBUTION OF INCOME AND WEALTH

The uninitiated in the intricacies of the model of a market economy might easily be led to believe that it implies a unique equilibrium collection of goods or commodities produced and traded, associated with a unique distribution of income (of claims on the flow of the aggregate social product). Nothing could be further from the truth.

True enough, the factors of production are bought and sold as commodities in the market, and their prices are determined along with the prices of all other commodities. But the equilibrium solution of the system (which yields the equilibrium set of prices and the equilibrium collection of goods produced and traded) cannot be determined without a specification of the initial distribution of claims on the economy's resources. The reason is that the quantities of factors of production supplied in the market by a household, as well as the quantities of products demanded by it, depend on its initial wealth. And the pattern of household demands for final products along with the pattern of factor supplies is directly dependent upon the initial distribution of wealth.

One must begin, therefore, by positing some initial distribution of wealth. Then, and only then, the model will grind out a solution—a set of equilibrium prices and a collection of commodities produced and traded in the market. Indeed, to each initial distribution of wealth there corresponds, in general, a different equilibrium set of prices and a different collection of commodities. It also follows from the very properties of our model, that each of the alternative general equilibria (corresponding to alternative initial distributions of wealth) is Pareto-optimal.

This formulation of the problem of distribution makes it possible for economists to be neutral vis-à-vis distribution questions. The orthodox line takes the following form: "If we ensure a Pareto-optimal solution, that is to say, an unbiased general equilibrium, we make sure that there is no waste in the economy, that we can make no one 'better off' without making someone 'worse off.' Once this is guaranteed, the question of distribution of income (wealth) can be considered, independently, on moral or on political grounds. We can leave such questions to the preacher or to the politician." But this will not do. On strictly technical grounds, any change in the distribution of income (wealth) by the politician implies a shift from one state of general equilibrium to another. The final outcome of the economic process (as depicted by the economist's model) is *not* separable from ethical-political decisions on income (wealth) distribution.

But there is a far more important consideration whose neglect by the main-line economists has been a source of significant bias in their policy recommendations. Social institutions, which form the basis for and the framework of economic activity, are intimately linked to patterns of distribution of wealth. There exists, in general, an organic relationship between social institutions (social structure) and the distribution of wealth. Although in each type of society there may exist some flexibility in this respect—that is, narrower or wider margins for tampering with the distribution of wealth —the general qualitative properties of wealth distribution are set. Sweden is an interesting case in point. While maintaining a capitalist social structure, it has pursued for decades income and wealth redistributive policies of socialist character. There is cumulative evidence that the limits of this process have been reached, that capitalist institutions there cannot be stretched any farther to accommodate an expansion of socialist policies.

Olof Palme's income redistributive policies ran into heavy weather when the elite of his civil service struck to prevent a narrowing of the income gap between blue-collar and white-collar workers. And this is quite apart from the difficulties he has been having in putting to rest the anxieties of the handful of families that control Sweden's weath. No government in the West can underestimate with impunity the capability of the Establishment to strike back when its interests are at stake. There is much the Establishment can do on its own. It can easily create a climate of fear and instability, with far-reaching effects on the rate of annual investment. It can redirect its investment to foreign opportunities in ways that may undermine the country's balance of payments. More than that, the home-based Establishment can claim the support of the international financial community, with a network of political and economic influence, in its struggle to undermine the policies of a government it deems hostile to its interests. The forthcoming elections in Sweden will undoubtedly shape up into a major confrontation between Palme's socialist policies and the Establishment's sustained effort to frustrate them. No matter what the outcome, one should not expect a continuation of the present fragile status quo. Instead one should expect either a return to more conservative, Establishment-oriented policies or a more determined socialization of Sweden's economy, involving a genuine qualitative change in the country's social structure.

Economists, in describing a market economy, assume in general, implicitly or explicitly, a set of social institutions which are identified with market capitalism. It goes without saying that radical redistribution policies would tend to come in conflict with the very institutional basis of market capitalism. (At the extreme, 100 per cent taxation amounts to expropriation). Thus, it is obvious that market capitalism cannot accommodate all patterns of distribution of wealth. The silence of economists on these matters, side by side with their assertion of neutrality vis-à-vis "ethical" problems, is a striking example of ideological bias.

More generally, the pursuit of certain distributional or employment objectives by the public policy authority often takes the form of intervention in the workings of the market economy. Price supports for agricultural products is a good case in point. Economists argue that this is an inefficient way of subsidizing farmers' incomes. (And it is in reference to the requirements of the model of the market economy.) To escape this criticism the policy authority should, in fact, leave prices alone and make outright grants to farmers in a fashion such that their relative subjective valuations between leisure and work will not be changed. Is it any wonder that governments are not prepared to accept such prescriptions?

In fact, the institutional framework of each society places

distinct limitations on the manner in which wealth and income distribution policies can be pursued. And in view of these limitations, the adoption of an income redistribution policy may lead to inefficiency in terms of the requirements of and the assumptions implicit in the model. But this way of thinking ignores the fact that *efficiency* refers to the manner in which a set of goals are achieved. If they are achieved in a nonwasteful way, the process is efficient. If there exists a social preference for a particular pattern of income distribution, which can be achieved, say, only through a particular kind of social intervention, it is not legitimate to characterize the resulting resource allocation as inefficient.

But it is time to raise another question: Is the market economy, as historically experienced, so free of efficiency-distortions, that we are justified, when it comes to public policy decisions, in insisting on efficiency being assigned a primary, prepotent role?

*MONOPOLISTIC DEVIATIONS AND PIECEMEAL ANTITRUST

A monopolistic deviation from the model of a market economy takes the form of a violation of the parametric role of prices. A seller who is aware that through his sales he can affect the price of a commodity will take account of his influence on it in maximizing his profit. Such a seller is said to possess monopoly power. The price of the commodity is no longer a given bit of information for that seller, and the price system no longer plays the role attributed to it.

In can be proved easily that in a market economy with no monopolistic deviations every (firm) seller produces that quantity of a commodity which equates the market-given price of the commodity to his marginal cost.[5] This is a straight-

---

[5] Marginal cost is the increment to the firm's cost associated with producing an additional unit of the commodity.

forward result of maximizing profits.[6] Not surprisingly, it can also be shown that in a Pareto-optimal equilibrium, the prices of all commodities are equal to their marginal costs.[7]

But a firm wielding monoply power will have no interest in carrying production to the point where marginal cost equals the price of the commodity. The higher the quantity it produces, the lower the price. Price is no longer a measure of the incremental revenue to be gained by producing one more unit of the commodity. The rule of profit maximization now leads to the production of a lesser quantity than that which would equate marginal cost to price.[8] Thus monopoly power leads to an underutilization of resources in the production of the relevant commodity.

No economist doubts the almost universal presence of this type of monopoly power in the market economies of the West. Suffice it to say that the presence of any differentiation among products of the same technological type—be it on the basis of trademark, tradename and related advertising, or on the basis of location of retail outlets—constitutes a source of such monopoly power, the power to raise the price without losing all the customers. Therefore, no economist who accepts the standard model of the market economy and its intimate relation to an optimal or efficient state of affairs can doubt that the contemporary capitalist economies are imperfectly competitive and incorporate inefficiencies of unknown magnitude.[9]

[6] If the price of the commodity were greater than marginal cost, it would pay the firm to produce additional units; whereas if, the price were lower, it would pay to reduce production.

[7] Under special assumptions (namely, that factor supplies are fixed), a Pareto-optimal equilibrium implies only the proportionality of prices to marginal costs.

[8] Profit maximization in the case of monopoly implies the equalization of marginal cost to marginal (incremental) revenue. In monopolistic equilibrium, therefore, prices exceed marginal costs.

[9] Market capitalism in the presence of monopoly power has been characterized by main-line economists as monopolistically or imperfectly competitive capitalism; the suggestion being that the presence of monopoly power introduces flaws which lead to an admittedly unsatisfactory *variant* of market

It is fair to ask, How do economists deal with the policy implications of this generally recognized divergence between the requirements of the abstract model of a market economy and the ubiquitous presence of monopoly power?

We shall not be concerned here with the policy recommendations of economists who *reject* the competitive market economy model as a basis for their analysis and policy recommendations—concepts such as that of workable competition belong to a different ball game (this approach is considered in the next chapter). For an economist who sincerely accepts the full implications of the standard model of the market economy, three policy options are available. The first is a do-nothing policy. He might argue that such deviations from the model as exist are of secondary importance. Naturally, this constitutes an act of faith for, admittedly, it is exceedingly hard to obtain a measure of the inefficiency resulting from the ubiquitous presence of monopoly power in the economy. The second policy option is to call for an aggressive antitrust or antimonopoly activity on the part of the government. The objective in this case ought to be not only to break up the monopolies, but indeed to eliminate every vestige of monopoly power. Such a frontal attack on monopoly, however, is sure to destroy the institutional basis of capitalism. For it would be necessary, first, to eliminate all trademarks, tradenames, and advertising; and second, to break up all firms whose share of market is large enough to give them some influence over the product's price. It is certain, of course, that in many cases the large size of the firms would be justifiable on grounds of technological efficiency. To break them up would amount to destroying the technological basis of the economy as well. Thus

capitalism. In contrast the term *monopoly capitalism* (of Marxian or Neo-Marxian origin) as well as the term *paternalistic capitalism* (the main theme of this book) are intended to identify socioeconomic systems that, far from being simple variants of market capitalism, constitute distinct and contrasting systems.

this option, the option of "atomizing" the economy, can be rejected out of hand.

The third policy option is suggested by Oskar Lange's proposal for Market socialism.[10] In the Lange type of market socialism a Central Planning Board establishes a set of prices, searching for their equilibrium values through trial and error. Every firm manager is instructed to equate his marginal cost to the price ruling in the market—that is to say, he is instructed to act as if he were in a (competitive) market economy. This model of socialism, or alternatively, some model of a capitalist economy with centrally determined prices, is the logical terminal point for any economist who is sincerely committed to the efficiency-generating properties of the economy in the context of contemporary technology.

An objection could easily be raised against this Procrustean solution: Rather than acting as if monopoly power does not really matter or going all the way to an economy with centrally determined prices. Why not attack the more flagrant violations of competitive behavior, such as cartel agreements? Why not regulate or indeed take over only firms for which it is technologically natural to be monopolies, as in the case of public utilities? After all, can it not be claimed that piecemeal corrections of monopolistic deviations improve the state of affairs? But that is exactly the point. Surprisingly, the opposite can be proved: Namely, the correction of isolated monopolistic situations is most likely to make matters worse in terms of the kind of analysis that supports the model of a competitive market economy and the associated concept of a Pareto-optimum.

This is so because, as we know already, a Pareto-optimal equilibrium implies the proportionality of prices to marginal costs across the economy. In the case of a perfectly competitive

[10] See Oskar Lange and Fred M. Taylor, *On the Economic Theory of Socialism*, edited by Benjamin E. Lippincott (Minneapolis: University of Minnesota Press, 1938).

economy prices are equal to marginal costs, and the ratio of prices to marginal costs is equal to unity everywhere. In the presence of monopoly power prices exceed marginal costs, the ratio of price to marginal cost being a measure of the degree of monopoly power exercised by the firm. If by some accident all the firms in the economy happen to exercise the same degree of monopoly power, prices being proportional to marginal costs, then it would be true that no improvement in the allocation of resources could be brought about by intervention. Characteristically, in any contemporary capitalist economy, monopoly power is unevenly spread, and intervention is called for. But piecemeal intervention—intervention, say, intended to reduce the monopoly power of some particular firm by bringing the price of its product closer to its marginal cost—would be certain to constitute an improvement in the allocation of resources only if no other firm in the economy exercised monopoly power. In the presence of ubiquitous and unevenly spread monopoly power, it is possible that the reduction of the monopoly power of the firm in question would lead to a worsening of the situation. Indeed no intervention can be evaluated by itself, but only in reference to its overall impact on the spread of the ratios of prices to marginal costs in the economy.

Thus, for those who are committed to the model of the market economy only two policy options are truly open: either to wave the problem away or to adopt market socialism. (Or, alternatively, to adopt some model of a capitalist economy with prices determined by a central authority—in the Lange fashion.) To argue that monopolistic deviations can be ignored because of their minor importance is to exhibit ideological bias. To argue that piecemeal antitrust leads to improvements is false. The only bias-free option is the option that leads to a centrally controlled economy. But how many "believers" in fact are prepared to accept this conclusion?

*COSTS AND BENEFITS
EXTERNAL TO THE MARKET

Economists have been aware all along of the fact that the production or consumption of commodities may inflict damages or confer benefits to innocent bystanders in society which are not taken account of in their market prices. Equally, they have been aware that under such conditions equilibrium is not optimal.

The price of a product produced or consumed in a process that pollutes the air or the water or creates deafening noise for the inhabitants of the area in which it is located does not, in general, reflect the damages inflicted on innocent bystanders.[11] It has been the dominant custom of economists, however, to relegate the issue to footnotes until somewhat recently, when the furor over ecological imbalance and the miseries of urban life in the advanced industrialized societies gave the issue prominence in the news challenged only by major wars or major civil disturbances.

How do economists deal with this increasingly important issue? Specifically, what, if any, adjustments must be made to the model of a market economy to ensure that the resulting general equilibrium satisfies the conditions of optimality in the allocation of resources?

Let us suppose, taking a very simple case, that the adverse external effects are associated with the production of coal in some community. The coal producer, in maximizing his profits, produces that quantity which equates his *private* marginal cost to the ruling price of coal in the market. This private marginal cost schedule, however, does not include an estimate of the damage inflicted by soot to the inhabitants of the neighborhood. Thus it is too low from a social point of view, and

---

[11] The discussion here will be limited to the case of external diseconomies. The case of external economies, though important for a range of problems, is not relevant to our concerns in this chapter.

leads to the production of a greater quantity of coal than is socially desirable. Now, if the soot damage were included in the coal producer's marginal cost schedule, it would transform it into a *social* marginal cost schedule. If the coal producer were to select that quantity of coal which equalizes the social marginal cost to price, he would be producing the socially desirable amount of coal.

This example suggests that, in the face of external effects, the transformation of private into social marginal cost (for all firms in the economy)[12] ensures an optimal allocation of resources. Assuming that this is the case, we must next ask how this is to be achieved in a capitalist market economy.

The overwhelmingly impressive evidence of damaging externalities in our contemporary industrial society makes it inappropriate for the economist to slough off the question. The orthodox answer is conceptually very simple: indirect taxes can be devised in principle that will carry out this transformation. Actually, if the problem were limited to a few key industries, the government might undertake to collect the information necessary for instituting the appropriate tax schedules. The task would be no more difficult, say, than that involved in the regulation of public utilities. But damaging externalities are ubiquitous. Nothing less will do than an economy-wide structure of indirect taxes designed to transform private marginal costs into social marginal costs. But this task, informationally, imposes as much strain on the governmental authority as a detailed quantitative plan would impose on it in a planned economy. The informational economies guaranteed by decentralization in the market economy would suddenly disappear. Thus, for the advocates of a decentralized, competitive market economy this solution will not do.[13]

[12] I ignore here any external effects of *consuming* commodities.

[13] Recent efforts to solve the externalities problem by instituting markets for them through public action (i.e., markets in which firms may buy rights to degrees of pollution, etc.), though intellectually intriguing, are not likely to

But there is another possibility, that of letting each producer compensate those members of society on whom damages have been inflicted. This compensation transforms the producer's private marginal costs into social marginal costs in exactly the same way that indirect taxes do. But in this case the central political authority need not process huge amounts of data in order to arrive at an appropriate, economy-wide tax schedule. The exact levels of the injuries sustained and, therefore, of the compensations required, could be adjudicated by the courts in cases of conflict of opinion.[14]

The producers could easily object to this procedure. In fact, they could fall back on the economist's concept of optimality, and insist that they be bribed by the injured parties to reduce the quantity of the offensive product. From a resource-allocation point of view, this method of achieving the reduction in output is just as effective as compulsory compensation. Actually, the injured parties would be no worse off by bribing the producer to cut back production. Nor would the producer be worse off, since he would be compensated for his loss of profits.

This might seem to lead to embarrassing confusion, but the logic is actually quite simple. For the compulsory compensation solution implies that the property rights of the producers do not include the right to inflict damage on other parties. Alternatively, the solution whereby the injured parties bribe the firms would imply that the property rights of the producers do include the right to inflict such damage, that is to say, the right to pillage.

The legal content of property rights defines wealth. It does not call for much deep thinking to conclude that it is of the essence in a capitalist order to define property rights (wealth)

bear fruit, except in a few isolated cases. Furthermore, they do require some basic, initial regulatory decisions whose informational requirements may again turn out to be quite high.

[14] The information processing problem in such cases could be quite overwhelming. Often it is not possible to determine even the source of an injury, and determining its extent may turn out to be terribly costly.

in such a way as to give the producer the upper hand. Thus the bribe case is genuinely a capitalist case. The compulsory compensation case, in contrast, if generally applied would tend to undermine the institutional foundations of capitalist society. Genuine concern over the external effects of the contemporary industrial process—with their devastating impact on the environment and the quality of life—forces us to look for solutions outside the main-line economist's model of the market economy. For it is hard to avoid the conclusion that effective confrontation of the problem leads either to large-scale regulation or to the *internalization* of externalities through reliance on some form of social planning.

*PUBLIC GOODS AND THE ROLE ASSIGNED TO THE STATE

The model of the market capitalism faces one of its severest tests when it becomes necessary to rationalize the role of the contemporary state, and along with it the institutional structure that provides the necessary framework for the carrying on of economic activity. For the orthodox it is an onerous and unpleasant task to explain why anything more is needed than a simple legal-institutional framework with provisions concerning property rights and the rules governing exchange. This is not surprising. The nominalist view of society that provides the philosophical underpinnings of market capitalism relegates the State to the status of a necessary evil, an unfortunate but inescapable afterthought.

The concept of public goods is the economist's entrance ticket to the theory of the state. Unwilling to grant emergent properties to society—and insisting through thick and thin to viewing it as an aggregation of individuals—he seeks the raison d'être of the State in the inherent properties of certain types of goods.

The Myth of Market Capitalism

Robert Dorfman, representing a widely held view, states that, "there are certain goods that have the peculiarity that once they are available no one can be precluded from enjoying them whether he contributed to their provision or not. These are the public goods. Law and order is an example, and there are many others too familiar to make further exemplification worth while. Their essential characteristic is that they are enjoyed but not consumed (and that their benefits are derived) without any act of appropriation."[15] But this definition can be rephrased: public goods are goods that must be provided publicly (by the state) because the market mechanism is incapable of performing its allocative functions. Is this really more than an apologetic admission of defeat?

But Dorfman's definition of public goods is limited to what have come to be called "perfect collective consumption goods." These are goods (such as law and order and national defense) associated with a complete breakdown of the allocative capabilities of the private property–market–exchange apparatus. It is known, of course, that there exists an impressive array of goods and services provided by the state which do not meet Dorfman's definition of public goods: public education, public power, irrigation, and so on. In all these instances, it is possible to exclude classes of individuals from participation in their enjoyment, since it is possible to make them available at a charge. And clearly, in at least some of these instances, such goods may be provided privately through the operation of the market mechanism. Thus, the decision to provide them publicly, rather than privately through the market mechanism, must be based on grounds other than their inherent properties.

There seems to be no escape from the conclusion that goods are provided publicly—and thus become public goods—whenever the market is incapable of providing them privately or

---

[15] "General Equilibrium with Public Goods," *Economie Publique*, a conference at Biarritz, September 2–9, 1966 (Paris: Centre National de la Recherche Scientifique, 1968), pp. 49–79.

when it provides them in a manner that is deemed unsatisfactory. (The unsatisfactory aspect of their private provision may relate to monopolistic deviations, to external effects, or to income distribution.) Notwithstanding the fact that this conclusion assigns a residual role to public activity, it contains a recognition of the possibility of large-scale failure of the market economy in providing certain types of goods or in providing other types of goods satisfactorily.

We come up against the inescapable question, Satisfactory or unsatisfactory to whom? Obviously, to the State, which engages in the provision of the public goods. But in whose interest does the State decide? And through what mechanism are its decisions affected by those whose interest it is intended to serve?

At this stage of the argument it is enough to point to the great cleavage of thought between the nominalist and the organicist points of view. The orthodox economist is clearly nominalist. According to this position public goods are provided when markets fail to satisfy individual demands. There is no place here for social as against private demands. Every social demand is decomposable into private demands. This approach creates no problem when the provision of a public good takes the form of an intervention of the State to correct market performance in the case of monopolistic deviations or of external effects because in both cases the intervention is intended to satisfy individual demands. Furthermore, it is distribution-neutral. But what about the provision of public goods in the Dorfman sense (law and order, national defense, the provision of an adequate resource base for future generations)? Are such demands *private*? To treat them as if they were, to include quantities of defense, law and order, and so on as arguments in the preference functions or preference rankings of individuals would stretch the term *private* beyond the breaking point. And what about the provision of a public good which carries with it a redistribution of income or wealth via the financing of its cost or via the allocation of its benefits? Most public goods (including law and order and national defense) clearly have distributive impacts. Some individuals become better off and others become worse off following their provision by the state. Who is to judge whether or not they should be provided? And on what grounds?

It seems inescapable that such decisions must be based on explicit social priorities. Recognition of the need for the articulation of social priorities in the domain of public action unavoidably leads to consideration of the emergent properties of society—to a view of society which streses its organic or systemic character.

Of course, one can shift the arena of the debate and attempt an extension of the nominalist view to the theory of the State, by defining the political process as a market-like process, where the votes replace the dollars. Some extremely intriguing attempts in this direction have been made. It is not surprising, however, that "all attempts to work out voting systems through which the population should be able to determine government activity and taxation in such a way that a perfect analogy with usual demand and payment for commodities is established have broken down.[16] Kenneth Arrow in a pioneering study[17] has demonstrated a paradox: whereas each individual in a group may have well-defined (consistent) preferences, it may well be impossible to derive a consistent group preference. Suppose, for instance, that individual 1 prefers candidate A to candidate C, and candidate C to candidate B; that individual 2 prefers C to B, and B to A; and that individual 3 prefers B to A, and A to C. Let us see now what happens to group (majority) preferences. A majority prefers candidate A to candidate C. A majority also prefers candidate C to candidate B. Yet, if the choice

[16] Bent Hansen, *Lectures in Economic Theory* (Lund: Student-litteratur, 1967), Pt. 2, p. 93.
[17] *Social Choice and Individual Values*, 2nd ed. (New York: Wiley, 1963).

33

is between candidate B and candidate A, the majority would prefer B. Peter Steiner, commenting on the analogy between the market mechanism and the voting process, sums up its weaknesses as follows: "(1) Voting involves an extra dimension of uncertainty: consequences follow the collective vote, not the individual vote; therefore, the voter may not really vote his own best interests because he underestimates the possibility of the decision impinging on him. Indeed since in a collective vote there is a diffusion of responsibility for the collective decision, the individual may act in the mass as he would never act individually. A man may vote for prohibition, for capital punishment, or for a war policy while at the same time he would not abstain from alcohol, invoke the death sentence, or opt for military service for himself or his son. (2) In voting, the individual is influenced by his sense of participation in social choice. A vote for open housing need not imply a willingness to live in a racially mixed neighborhood: indeed many of the most ardent supporters of such laws have exercised their option to move further away from integrated neighborhoods. Men may be willing to do collectively unto others what they would not do individually nor consent to have done to them unless done to all. (3) In voting, the individual is often faced with indivisible votes for mutually exclusive choices. He cannot make marginal choices, or influence very much the definition of candidate or choices. Often he votes for candidates some of whose policies he disapproves. Thus the mandate of a winning candidate is readily misinterpreted. (4) Minority votes are wasted, whereas even minority preferences exert influences in the market. If fear of wasting their votes leads voters to vote for their second choices, even the actual votes for candidates may fail to reflect the strength of the support their views have. Non-voting, an alternative form of expression is not often easily interpreted. . . . These critiques . . . serve to warn against too quick acceptance of an analogy of the political process with the market process. The practical question is whether the two situations are sufficiently similar that the economist's techniques of analysis . . . can be applied directly and fruitfully to political decision making. My own answer . . . is 'No.' "[18]

It is difficult to avoid the conclusion that the State must be viewed as an "organic chooser of ends" in the context of a political process whose nature, though different from case to case, makes it much more than a passive receiver of signals from a voting constituency or a mediating instrumentality that aggregates private into public demands. The traditional nominalist view of public goods and of the role of the State does not fit the experience of any society, much less that of our own. It springs from a healthy concern over the arbitrary authority of an ever-expanding state. But, by ignoring the role of the political process—which constitutes an integral part of the mechanism of resource allocation—it lends support to the convenient rationalization that in "democratic" societies, the State does exactly what is wanted by the people. Thus, the attempts by the orthodox nominalists to minimize the role of the State in their models is grist for the mill of the vested interests that employ the machinery of the state to their own advantage, in absentia of the liberal intellectual. Once again ideological bias, unwittingly, becomes the servant of the status quo.

*CREATIVE DESTRUCTION VERSUS ADMINISTRATION

Whether one reads Schumpeter or Marx, and whether one is led to view capitalism as an innovative process of creative

[18] "The Public Sector and the Public Interest," in *The Analysis and Evaluation of Public Expenditures: The PPB System: A Compendium of Papers Submitted to the Subcommittee on Economy in Government of the Joint Economic Committee, Congress of the United States* (Washington, D.C.: GPO, 1969), pp. 37–38. Steiner's argument in this instance is based on J. M. Buchanan, "Individual Choice in Voting and the Market," *Journal of Political Economy*, Vol. 62, August 1954, pp. 334–343.

35

destruction or as a process of capital accumulation, one is necessarily forced to view it as an evolutionary process. Not a trace of this evolutionary—one could say, revolutionary—dynamic of capitalism remains in the standard model of market capitalism. For clearly, neoclassical economics is an elaborate but expurgated version of the economics of the great thinkers of the nineteenth century.

To use Schumpeter's felicitous distinction, neoclassical economics is concerned with the *administrative* rather than the *creative* aspects of the economic process. The fundamental problem to be solved is how best to allocate known scarce resources among competing independently articulated individual ends, in the light of a known technology. This is fundamentally a managerial problem—even though, of course, no manager is in evidence. Thus the emphasis here is on the allocative properties of a market economy in a static, non-dynamic, nonevolutionary context. Certainly economists have been increasingly concerned with the dynamic, intertemporal allocation of resources. The difficulty encountered in extending the efficiency properties of the market economy in the static context to the dynamic, intertemporal context is the absence of futures markets side by side with spot markets, for all but a few commodities (such as foreign exchange and a few internationally traded standardized commodities). But this is only part of the problem because the intertemporal resource allocation process is an integral part of change in the underlying structure. Everything is in flux. The individuals that make up society, their tastes, the known resources, the shopping list of products, the technology to be employed, the supporting institutions, all are in a state of flux. Although this evolutionary process is enormously difficult to comprehend, let alone formalize, one is quite irresponsible to ignore it or to push it out of the social scientist's field of vision. But this is exactly what economists

The Myth of Market Capitalism

do by restricting their attention to problems of resource management in a nonevolutionary context.

What in fact is truly impressive about the capitalist evolutionary process is its directional indeterminacy. E. J. Mishan has written an entertaining parable which brings out forcefully this indeterminacy in the direction of the process. It also suggests the extent to which the limited or "marginal" social vision so characteristic of capitalist economies, buttressed by strongly entrenched vested interests, creates an ironclad bondage for society. ". . . without straining his credulity perhaps, the reader may be able to picture to himself a region of some continent, say, on the other side of the Atlantic in which the traditional right to carry firearms is never questioned. Indeed, on the initiative of the manufacturers, who spend colossal sums in advertising their new wares, more than one pistol is to be seen in a man's belt. The young men in particular are anxious to be seen with the latest de luxe 'extra hard-hitting' model. Obviously the manufacture of holsters and other accessories flourishes as also does the manufacture of bullet-proof vests, leggings and helmets. These are not the only growth industries, however, for notwithstanding the purchase of bullet-proof items, the members of the undertakers' association do a flourishing trade. The windows of all but the poorer houses are fitted with shatter-proof glass, while the bullet-proofing of rooms and offices in the more dangerous districts is a matter of ordinary precautions. No family is foolish enough to neglect the training of their sons, and even their daughters, in the art of the quick draw. In any case, a number of hours each week is devoted to target practice and dodgery in all the best schools. Life insurance is, of course, big business despite the exorbitant premiums, and expenditure on medical attention continues to soar. For in addition to such normal ailments as bullets embedded in various parts of the anatomy, there is widespread suffering from a variety of chafed skin diseases, the result of wearing the unavoidably heavy bullet-proof apparel. Moreover, owing to nervous diseases and anxiety, about every other adult is addicted either to strong liquor or to tranquilizing drugs. Taxes are burdensome for obvious reasons: a swollen police force employed mainly in trying to keep down the number of victims of the perennial feud, extensive prisons and prison hospitals, to say nothing of the public funds devoted to guarding offices, banks, schools, and to the construction of special vans for transporting the children to and from schools.

"In such an environment the most peace-loving man would be foolish to venture abroad unarmed. And since it is observed by the *laissez-faire* economist that men freely choose to buy guns, it would be regarded as an infringement of liberty to attempt to curb their manufacture. Moreover, since the market is working smoothly, the supply of firearms being such that no one need wait if he is able to pay the market price, no government intervention to match industrial supplies to rising demand is called for. Provided there is enough competition in the production of firearms so that over the long period prices just cover costs (and tend also to equal marginal costs of production) the allocation economist is well satisfied. Looking at the promising signs of growth in the chief industries, the firearms and accessories, the business economist pronounces the economy 'sound.' If, however, for any reason the Government begins to have misgivings about some of the more blatant repercussions, it consults with the pistol economist, a highly paid and highly regarded expert. The pistol economist constructs models and, with the help of high-powered statisticians, amasses pistological data of all kinds, from which he calculates the optimal set of taxes on the sale of pistols and ammunition in recognition of those external diseconomies, such as occasional corpse-congestion on the better streets, whose monetary costs can, he believes, be estimated.

"Notwithstanding all his scientific advice, matters eventually come to a head, and amid much government fanfare a committee of inquiry is set up under the chairmanship of a highly competent engineer, Mr. B. If there ever was a realist, Mr. B. is one, and he soon satisfies himself that the economy is heavily dependent upon pistol production, and all the auxiliary industries and services connected therewith. Besides, the evidence is incontrovertible: the demand for guns continues to grow year by year. It must, therefore, be accepted as a datum. Undaunted, Mr. B. faces the 'challenge' by proposing a radical remodelling of the chief towns and cities, at an unmentionable cost, in the endeavour to create an environment in which people can have both their guns and a peaceful life as well. The chief features of his plan are based on what he aptly calls 'pistol architecture,' and includes provision for no-shooting precincts fenced high with steel, the construction of circular and wavy road design to increase the difficulties of gun-duelling, the erection of high shatter-proof glass screens running down the centres of roads to prevent effective cross-firing, and the setting up of heavily protected television cameras at all strategic positions in the towns in order to relay information twenty-four hours a day to a vast new centralized police force equipped with fleets of helicopters. Every progressive journalist pays tribute to the foresight and realism of the B-plan and makes much of the virtues of 'pistol architecture,' the architecture of the future. Alas, the government begins to realize that any attempt to raise the taxes necessary to implement the B-plan would start a revolution. So the plan is quietly shelved, new committees of inquiry are formed, masses of agenda are produced, and things continue much as before."[19]

The parable should have made it quite clear that the study of the capitalist market economy, when restricted to the non-evolutionary aspects of the capitalist process, ceases to be rele-

[19] E. J. Mishan, *The Costs of Economic Growth* (Penguin Books, 1967), pp. 125–127.

vant to it. Expurgated and anemic, it throws more light on the performance of an ideal society of shopkeepers than on contemporary capitalism. To extend, unwittingly or not, the analytical conclusions of a model best fitted for the study of a shopkeeper society to present-day capitalism is probably the supreme form of ideological bias.

A Neo-Marxist View
of the Capitalist
Metropolis

If contemporary capitalism is not a society of competing shopkeepers, then what is it? Ever since James Burnham's *The Managerial Revolution* or even A. A. Berle's and G. C. Means' *The Modern Corporation and Private Property* there have been many attempts to propose an alternative, more "realistic" view of contemporary capitalism. Of these, today two stand out. The first, a Neo-Marxist interpretation, is Paul Baran and Paul Sweezy's *Monopoly Capital*.[1] The second is J. K. Galbraith's *The New Industrial State*.[2] It is clear that no meaningful discussion of contemporary, advanced-country capitalism can go forward without reference to these two closely related formulations.

*THE SURPLUS

The Baran-Sweezy formulation "is organized and attains its essential unity from one central theme: the generation and absorption of the surplus under conditions of monopoly capitalism."[3] The authors make it clear that the "surplus" is

[1] New York & London: Modern Reader Paperbacks, 1966.
[2] London: Hamish Hamilton, 1967; Boston: Houghton Mifflin, 1967; also available as a Signet Book (New York: New American Library, 1968).
[3] *Monopoly Capital*, p. 8.

41

equivalent to Marx's "surplus value."[4] But "in a highly developed monopoly capitalist society, the surplus assumes many forms and disguises. . . . It is for this reason that we prefer the concept 'surplus' to the traditional Marxian 'surplus value,' since the latter is probably identified in the minds of most people familiar with Marxian economic theory as equal to the sum of profits + interest + rent." Baran and Sweezy define the term as follows: "The economic surplus, in the briefest possible definition, is the difference between what a society produces and the cost of producing it. The size of the surplus is an index of productivity and wealth, of how much freedom a society has to accomplish whatever goals it may set for itself. The composition of the surplus shows how it uses that freedom: how much it invests in expanding its productive capacity, how much it consumes in various forms, how much it wastes and in what ways."[5] Thus, to compute the surplus we must subtract from what a society produces the cost of producing it. What we come up with depends on the manner in which the minuend and the subtrahend are defined. The Baran-Sweezy definition does not directly resolve these questions. Naturally, one can fall back on the Marxian definition of surplus value. Or one can rely on the operational (statistical) definition given by J. D. Phillips in the appendix to *Monopoly Capital*. Phillips' surplus equals property income, plus all government expenditure, plus (an estimate of) waste in the business process (mainly the sales effort). "It should be noted, however, that these totals still do not include all elements of surplus. Some could not be estimated on a year-by-year basis because of inadequate data. One of these elements is the penetration

---

[4] Marx's surplus value is equal to the difference between the socially necessary labor-time incorporated in the commodities produced and the socially necessary labor-time incorporated in the commodities necessary for the subsistence (and reproduction) of the labor-power used in the process of production.

[5] *Monopoly Capital*, pp. 9–10.

of the productive process by the sales effort. . . . Another
element which might reasonably be incorporated in the surplus, but is omitted here, is the output foregone owing to the
existence of unemployment."[6]

All this lacks precision. The main reason lies in the fact
that waste and surplus are two entirely distinct concepts.
Unfortunately, Baran and Sweezy don't make this sufficiently
clear. It would be useful to sharpen the distinction. To do so,
we will fall back not on the standard United States or Western
definition of *national income*, nor indeed on the Russian definition, but on that provided by Harvard economist Simon
Kuznets. According to Kuznets, "we assume that the final goal
of economic activity is provision of goods to consumers, the
final products are those turned out during the year to flow
either to consumers or to capital stock (for the ultimate benefit of future consumers), and that everything else, by the
nature of the cases, is *intermediate product* whose inclusion
in the output total would constitute duplication."[7] And elsewhere, "national income is a measure of net output of economic activity *within* the given social framework, not what
it would be in a hypothetical absence of the latter. . . . In
other words, the flow of services to individuals from the
economy is a flow of economic goods produced and secured
under conditions of internal peace, external safety, and legal
protection of specific rights, *and cannot include these very
conditions as services*."[8] This definition of social product or
national income leads directly to the concept of social intermediate product or social cost. "Social cost is the cost of the

[6] *Ibid.*, p. 370. According to this definition, the surplus in the United States
was 46.9 per cent of GNP in 1929 and 56.1 per cent in 1963, and property
income was 57.5 per cent of surplus in 1929 and 31.9 per cent in 1963.
[7] "National Income: A New Version," *Review of Economics and Statistics*,
Vol. 30, No. 3, August 1948, pp. 151–179.
[8] Simon Kuznets, "Government Product and National Income," in Erik
Lundberg, ed., *Income and Wealth*, Ser. I (Cambridge: Bowes & Bowes,
1951), pp. 171–244.

entire social and economic organization of a particular society, the cost of a social system." It includes "all the non-investment government goods and services which do not enter directly into the consumption of individual consumers, . . . the services of the local bus company" when walking to the place of work is replaced by bus journeys, "the services of banks and other financial intermediaries,"[9] all activities associated with the sales effort, and many other possibly significant items. Thus, social cost includes both private and social resource uses relating to the support of a particular institutional structure or mode of social organization. It is clear that social cost is not a component of the social product (which is defined net of social cost in the Kuznets-Horvat context). Undeniably, the estimation of social product, thus defined, is a difficult task. The concept, however, is reasonably clear.

We may now ask: What component of the social product constitutes surplus? Clearly, all (private or social) investment and all (private or social) consumption in excess of necessary consumption constitute surplus.[10] For a definition of *necessary consumption*, we may turn directly to Baran. "Where living standards are in general low, and the basket of goods available to people little variegated, essential consumption can be circumscribed in terms of calories, other nutrients, quantities of clothing, fuel, dwelling space, and the like. Even where the level of consumption is relatively high, and involves a large variety of consumer goods and services, a judgment on the amount and composition of real income necessary for what is socially considered to be 'decent livelihood' can be made . . . this is precisely what has been done in all countries in emer-

[9] Branko Horvat, *Towards a Theory of Planned Economy* (Beograd: Yugoslav Institute of Economic Research, 1964), pp. 213–214.

[10] The estimates of consumption and investment must be consistent with the concept and method of measurement of social product. Their sum, in other words, must equal social product — and thus should not include any component of social cost.

gency situations such as war, postwar distress, and the like."[11]
It is clear that Baran's (and Marx's) definition of necessary
consumption is culture-related. But it should be stressed that
an unknown but undoubtedly significant component of
necessary consumption as defined by Baran must consist of
items that constitute social cost,[12] which must be deducted if
we are to arrive at a total consistent with the concept of social
product (along the Kuznets-Horvat lines).

But investment and unnecessary consumption do not ex-
haust surplus. We must add the total of social cost. Thus, the
surplus can be defined as the sum of unnecessary consumption,
of investment, and of the social cost.

But what is social waste, and how does it relate to the
surplus? Unfortunately, the concept of social waste is much
more elusive. We may get at it through a hypothetical experiment. Starting from the social product (in the Kuznets-Horvat
sense) of a given society, we may consider how the social
cost of that social product varies with alternative forms of
social organization. We carry this hypothetical investigation
far enough to discover the society (say, some socialist or communist society) for which the social cost is minimum. Next,
we subtract this minimum social cost from the actual social
cost of the society under investigation. The difference we call
the differential social cost of the society we are investigating.

We are now in a position to give a precise (though, unfortunately, hardly operational) definition of *social waste*: social
waste in any society is the differential social cost of that
society.

This excursion into the meanings of *surplus* and of *social
waste* makes it obvious that, far from being simple statistical

[11] Paul Baran, *The Political Economy of Growth* (New York & London:
Modern Reader Paperbacks, 1968), pp. 30–31.
[12] To the extent that for the U.S. wage-earner the automobile has become
a condition for earning a living, it represents social cost rather than consumption. Many other examples can be cited.

categories, they constitute devices intended to provide a quantitative tool for expressing, respectively, a society's freedom to employ resources in the pursuit of its ends, whatever these may be, and the extent or degree of irrationality in its ways of using resources.[13]

The essentially nonoperational character of the concepts of the surplus and of social waste does not render them useless, but it limits the way in which they can be used in social analysis. In the case of the concept of social waste a further question arises. Clearly, it implies a value judgment and a preference for social systems associated with lower social costs over those associated with higher social costs. A similar value judgment underlies the Kuznets-Horvat concept of social cost (or social intermediate product). One may wonder why this value judgment needs to be made. Is it not possible that the social system with the higher social cost might be preferred because of the quality of life it supports? And is it not legitimate to recognize social priorities which may not be reducible to individual wants or tastes?

In fairness to Baran and Sweezy, one should say that they do not develop a universal definition of social waste, as I have attempted to do here. The Baran-Sweezy argument is developed in the context of what they call monopoly capitalism. And it is their intent to make a value judgment, to argue that the uses made of the surplus in monopoly capitalism lead to waste—in the sense that they do not reflect articulated individual or social needs. Their point simply is that monopoly capitalism is profoundly irrational. But obviously this point could be made without the aid of the concept of surplus.

[13] Before closing this discussion, I should note that the inclusion in surplus of social product lost (wasted) as a result of unemployment of resources could be legitimated only if surplus and waste were measured in terms of potential rather than actual social product. We would then be forced to talk about potential surplus (which would be partly realized and partly not) — and the whole argument would become too fuzzy and esoteric to be of much interest.

*MONOPOLY CAPITALISM

Armed with the concept of surplus, Baran and Sweezy proceed to outline the main features of monopoly capitalism—that is, of contemporary capitalism in its most advanced form. The first building block of their model is the giant corporation in the United States, which constitutes the new prototype of the business firm. In the giant corporation control rests with a self-perpetuating management, "responsibility to the body of stockholders [being] for all practical purposes a dead letter." Furthermore, "each corporation aims at and normally achieves financial independence through the internal generation of funds which remain at the disposal of the management."[14]

Does the management-controlled giant corporation maximize profits (as is assumed in orthodox economic analysis) or does it serve broader social ends, having become "soulful"?[15] Baran and Sweezy subscribe neither to the view of the corporation as a socially responsible multiple-end-seeking institution nor to the orthodox profit maximization interpretation (because of its extreme requirements of unlimited rationality and availability of information). Instead, they adopt James Earley's position, which is a behavioristic reformulation of the profit-maximization postulate. His "behavioral postulate could best be briefly described as 'a systematic temporal search for highest

[14] *Monopoly Capital*, p. 16. The authors' emphasis on the financial independence of the modern corporation is exaggerated. The issue is taken up in the next chapter, in connection with a discussion of Galbraith's identical position.

[15] According to Carl Kaysen, "no longer the agent of proprietorship seeking to maximize return on investment, management sees itself as responsible to stockholders, employees, customers, the general public, and, perhaps most important, the firm itself as an institution. . . . From one point of view, this behavior can be termed responsible: there is no attempt to push off onto workers or the community at large part of the social costs of the enterprise. The modern corporation is a soulful corporation" ("The Social Significance of the Modern Corporation," *American Economic Review*, Vol. 47, No. 2, May 1957, pp. 313–319).

practicable profits.' "[16] Baran and Sweezy praise Earley's work, because by "stressing the 'limited informational and computational resources of the firm,' he makes clear that no assumption of complete knowledge is involved. . . . The firm always finds itself in a given historical situation, with limited knowledge of changing conditions. In this context it can never do more than improve its profit position. In practice, the search for 'maximum' profits can only be the search for the greatest *increase* in profits which is possible in a given situation, subject of course to the elementary proviso that the exploitation of today's profit opportunities must not ruin tomorrow's. This is all there is to the profit maximization principle, but it also happens to be all that is necessary to validate the 'economizing' behavior patterns which have been the very backbone of all serious economic theory for the last two centuries."[17]

Furthermore, since the modern giant corporation is better equipped than its ancestors to pursue a profit maximization policy, it may be expected to be a more effective profit maximizer than they were. This does not imply that there exist no important behavioral differences between the giant corporation and its antecedent, the small-scale business enterprise. The longer time horizon of the giant corporation and the rationalization of management generate a more conservative attitude toward risk taking. Other differences between the small-scale capitalist enterprise and the modern giant corporation relate to the manner in which profits are utilized and to the social climate that goes with managerial bureaucracy. The tycoon of old has been replaced by the company man.

The managerial bureaucracy, however, does not constitute a "separate, independent, or 'neutral' social class. . . . The fact is that the managerial stratum is the most active and influential part of the propertied class. . . . Far from being a sepa-

[16] A discussion paper in *American Economic Review*, Vol. 47, No. 2, May 1957, pp. 330–335.
[17] *Monopoly Capital*, p. 27.

rate class, they constitute in reality the leading echelon of the property-owning class." The company man's success coincides with the success of the corporation in which and for which he works. "The company man is dedicated to the advancement of his company. . . . The primary objectives of corporate policy—which are at the same time and inevitably the personal objectives of the corporate managers—are thus strength, rate of growth, and size. There is no general formula for quantifying or combining these objectives—nor is there any need for one. For they are reducible to the single common denominator of profitability. Profits provide the internal funds for expansion. Profits are the sinew and muscle of strength, which in turn gives access to outside funds if and when they are needed. Internal expansion, acquisition, and merger are the ways in which corporations grow, and growth is the road to size. Thus profits, even though not the ultimate goal, are the necessary means to all ultimate goals. As such, they become the immediate, unique, unifying, quantitative aim of corporate policies, the touchstone of corporate rationality, the measure of corporate success." [18]

This formulation of the propelling forces within the modern giant corporation is eminently sound. The nexus is profits through growth and growth through profits.

Baran and Sweezy's model relates to the management-controlled corporations, where external interest groups (say, financial institutions) do not exercise significant influence over their policies.

[18] *Ibid.*, pp. 34–35, 38, 39–40.

Although there is nothing iconoclastic in Baran and Sweezy's hypothesis about the controlling, propelling drive of the modern giant capitalist enterprise, the same cannot be said about their key hypothesis concerning the behavior of the system as a whole. It is in this connection that monopoly capitalism comes into its own.

I have already discussed the concept of monopolistic deviations from the model of market capitalism—deviations associated with the presence of monopoly power, the power to raise the price of a product without losing all customers. This power derives from two courses: first, from large size of a seller's output relative to total output placed on a market, and second, from differentiation of a seller's product from that of other sellers. (What matters in this connection is that the buyer, rightly or wrongly, perceives a seller's product as being different from that of other sellers.) Underlying both sources of monopoly power is the presence of obstacles or barriers to the entry of new competitors, free entry being fundamental to the preservation of the competitive character of a market. Clearly the two limiting polar cases are perfect competition and monopoly. The distinctive characteristic of the former is the inability of any seller in the market to affect the price through his actions. It obtains when each seller's share of the market is minuscule, his product undifferentiated, and entry of new sellers free. Monopoly is the case of just one seller in the market. It is generally supposed that public utilities are monopolies. And, presumably for this reason, they are directly regulated by governments.

No one has suggested that contemporary capitalism is monopolistic in this sense, that it is an economy of monopolies, each market being dominated by just one firm. But all economists accept that in the key markets of the contemporary capitalist economy just a few firms are dominant. Such markets, markets supplied by just a few dominant sellers, are called oligopolistic and the dominant sellers oligopolists. Each oligopolist is capable of affecting the price of the product, but what he does affects each and every other oligopolist in the market. Thus, in making a decision, an oligopolist must take account of his competitors' reaction to his moves. This is characteristically, then, a situation to be understood in terms of games of strategy. The arsenal of each oligopolist includes price, quality of product, advertising, control of marketing channels, and so forth. How these weapons will be used by an oligopolist depends on his strategy—an aggressive, cutthroat strategy or a cooperative, live-and-let-live, collusive one. The former is exemplified by price wars among oligopolists intended to lead to a reallocation of shares of the market among the survivors. The latter is exemplified by the cartel, where the oligopolists collude and act as if they were a joint monopoly.

Economists consider both polar types of oligopolistic behavior, the price war and the cartel, as highly undesirable—the price war because it leads to the victory of the strongest and, therefore, to monopoly; the latter because it is monopoly. Antitrust legislation is generally supposed to be aimed at limiting both polar forms of behavior. But to what end? If oligopolists are prevented from engaging in outright price wars and in outright collusion, they must be forced into some other kind of strategy. Is there some strategy which, if adopted by the oligopolists, could be considered socially desirable or acceptable?

Before proceeding to the answer, it is useful to note that, quite independently of the strategies followed by the oligopolists, the allocation of resources in oligopolistic markets will not be optimal (in the Pareto sense). Thus, in looking for socially acceptable oligopolistic strategies, economists are no longer talking within the framework of the basic model (discussed in the preceding chapter). They are talking, rather, within the framework of what has come to be called workable competition. This framework—no longer dealing with optima of any kind—is supposed to permit a search for those oligopolistic strategies which lead to socially acceptable results. Once defined, such strategies presumably should be encouraged by appropriate legislation.

Although there has been considerable work along these lines, the results and even the meaning of workable competition remain vague. For workable competition is, of necessity, a mixture of analytical insights and of ad hoc prescriptions. To begin with, some content must be given to the notion of social desirability or acceptability. Generally, a strategy or a behavior pattern is considered socially acceptable if on balance it leads to improvements in the quality of the products put on the market, to technological innovation and cost reductions, to a reduction of wasteful resource-using activities, and so forth. Some patterns of behavior, such as predatory price wars and outright collusion, are easily judged to be socially unacceptable on the basis of such criteria. For more subtle forms of oligopolistic behavior, however, it may be hard to obtain general agreement. For example, whether a merger of two large firms is acceptable or not may be said to depend on whether or not the power bestowed by the merger on the new unit vis-à-vis its oligopolistic competitors leads to a significant reduction of actual or potential competitive pressures on it. However, the acceptability may also be said to depend on the impact of the merger on the costs of production (through realization of economies of scale), on research, on the development of new products, and so forth. Much room is left for argument even among economists who accept the same ultimate criteria as to what is socially acceptable.

Thus, the pragmatic approach fostered by the concept of workable competition has led to a basically permissive and tolerant attitude vis-à-vis the oligopolistic world of contemporary capitalism. Most economists can point to the rising standard of living, to the continuous improvement of the products at the disposal of the citizen, to the technological wonders of our era, and argue that after all oligopolistic markets work pretty well. Let us pursue this a bit further.

Most economists agree on the most likely mode of behavior or strategy for a firm operating in an oligopolistic market and within a legal (antitrust) framework that prevents outright collusion and predatory price wars. Robert Dorfman summarizes the argument in a straightforward manner. "Beaten by the bench, and anxious to avoid further scrutiny and unfavorable publicity, oligopolists were forced to rely on more circumspect methods of cooperation. These depended heavily . . . on the observance and enforcement of unwritten behavioral conventions. The most ubiquitous of these conventions was that price competition was disallowed—and to this day oligopolists contest bitterly with each other by advertising, by product variation, by expense-account entertainment, by industrial espionage, and by every other expedient that ingenuity can invent, but they do not cut prices. Price-cutting is a weapon that is too readily available, and too destructive to all concerned. . . . By far the most common way to handle the matter is through the convention of price leadership: one prominent firm, often but not always the largest in the industry, is accepted as the one with the responsibility for initiating price changes for all to follow. . . . The continued maintenance of the leader's reign depends heavily on general acquiescence in the current distribution of market shares; when some of the firms vie vigorously to improve their positions in the market, or struggle desperately to survive, the peace is likely to be fragile. . . . A plausible hypothesis, though one very hard to confirm, is that the price leaders act like monopolists on behalf of the entire industry." [19]

[19] *Prices and Markets*, pp. 108–109. The emphasis is mine.

This statement of what is likely to happen in oligopolistic markets is unexceptional. Indeed, Baran and Sweezy's interpretation is to all intents and purposes equivalent to Dorfman's: "With price competition banned, sellers of a given commodity or of close substitutes have an interest in seeing that the price or prices established are such as to maximize the profits of the group as a whole. They may fight over the division of these profits . . . but none can wish that the total to be brought over should be smaller rather than larger. This is the decisive fact in determining the price policies and strategies of the typical large corporation. . . . Secret collusion is undoubtedly common, but it has its drawbacks and risks, and can hardly be described as the norm toward which a typical oligopolistic industry tends. That norm, it seems clear, is a kind of tacit collusion which reaches its most developed form in what is known as 'price leadership.' . . . So long as all firms accept this convention . . . it becomes relatively easy for the group as a whole to feel its way toward the price which maximizes the industry's profit. What is required is simply that the initiator of change should act with the group interest as well as its own interest in mind and that the others should be ready to signal their agreement or disagreement by following or standing pat. If these conditions are satisfied, we can safely assume that the price established at any time is a reasonable approximation to the theoretical monopoly price." [20]

One is entitled to think that the main-line economists (represented in this instance by Dorfman) and the Neo-Marxists (Baran and Sweezy), having adopted the same interpretation of the behavior of oligopolistic markets—the markets that dominate contemporary, advanced capitalism—would be forced to reach the same conclusions concerning its implications on the performance of the capitalist economy. But this is not the case.

[20] *Monopoly Capital*, pp. 59–62.

A Neo-Marxist View

For Baran and Sweezy, "it means that the appropriate general price theory for an economy dominated by such corporations is the traditional monopoly price theory of classical and neo-classical economies. What economists have hitherto treated as a special case turns out to be, under monopoly capitalism, the general case." [21] For Dorfman "Oligopoly is almost inevitable in industries that rely on modern technology . . . obviously it is far from an ideal state of affairs—but then, social institutions do have ways of adapting themselves to such challenges, and oligopoly is no exception. . . . In a clumsy way an oligopolistic industry retains a rough contact with the conditions of production and the desires of its customers. . . . Oligopolistic industries, in spite of their sluggishness, *behave tolerably like competitive ones* so long as the oligopolists do not collude with each other. *The government inhibits collusion through its antitrust policy and relies on oligopolistic industries, under mild supervision, to approximate competitive conditions.*" [22]

Thus for Dorfman oligopolistic industries "behave tolerably like competitive ones"—and this despite the fact that "a plausible hypothesis . . . is that the price leaders act like monopolists on behalf of the entire industry." This explicit and resounding contradiction in Dorfman's position results from the pragmatic and permissive attitude fostered by the concept of workable competition, a concept that almost inevitably leads to the acceptance of the "facts of life" as tolerable approximations to a competitive state of affairs whose virtues can be "rigorously" established. Thus, it is rather obvious that—at least with respect to the determination of prices in oligopolistic markets—Baran and Sweezy win the argument hands down. If one must choose between the competitive model and the monopo-

[21] *Ibid.*, p. 59.
[22] *Prices and Markets*, pp. 108–109, 140. The emphasis is mine.

ly one for predicting the price behavior of oligopolistic markets, one must choose the monopoly model.[23]

* * * * *

Baran and Sweezy consider the traditional theory of monopoly as adequate only in explaining price behavior in oligopolistic markets. "The abandonment of price competition does not mean the end of all competition: it takes new forms and rages on with ever increasing intensity. Most of these new forms of competition come under the heading of what we will call the sales effort." [24] In this the authors adopt the dominant, established view that non–price competition in oligopolistic markets is quite intensive. In fact, they tend to overemphasize this intensity, neglecting the well-known fact that even non–price competition in the contemporary economy of giant corporations is subject to a variety of important conventions that limit its impact on market shares and prevent sudden, dramatic changes in the relative position of the main contestants. (The relative size of the advertising budget, the rate of introduction of new models, and other dimensions of non–price competition are regulated by subtle but tenacious industry-wide conventions.)

Thus, Baran and Sweezy paint an image of behavior that combines monopoly in respect to price with aggressive, unbridled competition in respect to all other dimensions. This particular mix of behavior is essential to their argument because

---

[23] Later I shall show that another interpretation of the behavior of oligopolistic markets is possible—an interpretation that is similar to but not identical with that of Sweezy and Baran.

[24] Monopoly Capital, p. 67.

aggressive, unbridled non–price competition defines the "dynamics of market sharing." The drive for a greater share of the market—channeled primarily through the sales effort—implies a drive to reduce costs. The lower an oligopolist's costs, the better is his defense posture and the greater is his capability to engage in price war, if the dreaded moment comes. Thus, the oligopolists are driven not only to cut their costs but to do so faster than their rivals.[25] But it is unlikely that these cost reductions will be passed on to the consumer, since the oligopolists behave as a joint monopoly with respect to price. "This means that under monopoly capitalism, declining costs imply continuously widening profit margins. And continuously widening profit margins imply aggregate profits which rise not only absolutely but as a share of national product. If we provisionally equate aggregate profits with society's economic surplus, we can formulate as a law of monopoly capitalism that the surplus tends to rise both absolutely and relatively as the system develops." This law is crucial to the authors' edifice.[26]

No one is prepared to deny that oligopolists are engaged in introducing cost-reducing technologies, but the suggested intensity and scope of this cost-reducing activity may be questioned. It should not be forgotten that oligopolists are also busily engaged in insulating their share of the market and profits from potential competitive pressure through a variety of means which have little to do with cutting costs. And to the extent that they are successful, they are relieved of the need to

[25] The drive to cut costs is reinforced by the special form that the sales effort takes for oligopolists in producer goods industries. The buyers of such goods are sophisticated oligopolists who are not likely to be sold unless the goods supplied do in fact contribute to an increase in their profits through reduction in their costs.

[26] *Monopoly Capital*, pp. 71–72. One must exercise caution in interpreting the phrase "if we provisionally equate aggregate profits with society's economic surplus." It should be read to mean: "if we treat society's economic surplus as if it were aggregate profits." For according to the authors, one should not identify "recorded profits with the theoretical 'share of profit.' The latter is really what we call surplus, the difference between total output and the socially necessary costs of producing total output" (p. 76).

continuously revolutionize their technologies in order to cut costs. In fact, to the extent that non–price competition is itself subjected to conventions that normally bind the oligopolist competitors to certain patterns of behavior (affecting, say, the size of the advertising budget or the rate at which new models are introduced), the cost-cutting drive may be somewhat blunted.

The "law" of the tendency of surplus to rise is undermined, of course, by the possibility that labor unions may be "strong enough to capture for their members increments in profits resulting from the combination of declining costs and monopoly pricing." [27] Baran and Sweezy reject this possibility. "Unions certainly do play an important role in the determination of money wages, and the workers in more strongly organized industries generally do better for themselves than workers in less strongly organized branches of the economy. This does not mean, however, that the working class as a whole is in a position to encroach on surplus or even to capture increments of surplus, which, if realized, would benefit the capitalist class relative to the working class. The reason is that under monopoly capitalism employers can and do pass on higher labor costs in the form of higher prices. They are, in other words, able to protect their profit margins in the face of higher wages (and fringe benefits). In many cases in recent years, indeed, they have been able to weave wage increases into their monopoly pricing policies in such a way as to achieve a prompter and closer approach to the theoretical monopoly price than would otherwise have been possible." [28] The authors do not elaborate on this position. It is possible, however, to derive some of its implications. Although it may be true that the power of the unions to encroach on surplus of the corporate giants is nil or very limited, the same does not hold for less fortunate mem-

---

[27] Ibid., p. 77.
[28] Ibid.

bers of the business establishment. Monopoly power is not equally distributed over the population of enterprises. Thus, unions' actions may lead to a redistribution of surplus in favor of the corporate giants. And they do, of course, also lead to a redistribution of the wage share in favor of strong unions and, more generally, in favor of unionized labor. Thus it is sensible to talk about collusion between strong labor unions and the giant corporate establishments.

There arises, of course, the more basic question, Has the standard of living of the average worker in contemporary capitalist economies improved? And the answer is that it has. Baran and Sweezy surely are not prepared to deny this. How is this possible in Marxist terms, unless some encroachment on surplus has taken place?[29] The proper Marxist answer would have to be that the increase in the standard of living reflects the increasing social cost of performing the duties of a wage earner in an increasingly complex society. No doubt some component of the higher standard of living is absorbed by social cost. But it is equally true that some part of it is "enjoyed" by the recipients. The automobile may be necessary to a modern worker in the performance of his tasks, but it does give him the opportunity to take an occasional fishing trip.

It is operationally extremely difficult to differentiate between the component of the statistically measurable increase in the standard of living that reflects increases in the social cost of supplying a properly trained and properly motivated wage earner and the component that represents a genuine encroachment upon the surplus. Actually, the distinction may turn out not to be terribly important, for the system seems to face an increasingly difficult problem of disposing the surplus it generates in ways which do not undermine its social foundations. Thus encroachments upon the surplus by wage

---

[29] For in strict Marxist terms all increases in productivity are appropriated by the capitalists, since the working class earns just enough to subsist.

earners (or by salaried white-collar personnel) may well be consistent with the dynamics of the contemporary capitalist system, provided they lead to predictable increments in unnecessary consumption. Indeed, the development of consumer credit, side by side with feudal consumption requirements (type of house, proper location, type of car used, etc.) imposed on personnel by corporate managements create a tenacious form of social bondage for the working class, a bondage that strengthens the social foundations of the system as a whole. Indeed, one might wish to stretch the argument a bit further and claim that the encroachments upon surplus value by the working class which are directly tied to predictable increments in unnecessary consumption constitute—from the point of view of the system—a component of the overall social cost of maintaining its social foundations intact by providing meaningful outlets for expanding surplus.

How will the system dispose of its growing surplus? The very definition of the concept suggests the ways: it can be invested, it can be consumed (through increases in "unnecessary" consumption), and it can be wasted. Baran and Sweezy conclude that the capitalist system does not provide "investment outlets large enough to absorb a rising share of surplus." [30] Thus, the very survival of the system depends on developing effective "wasteful" ways for absorbing surplus. "Since surplus which cannot be absorbed will not be produced, it follows that the *normal* state of the monopoly capitalist economy

[30] *Monopoly Capital*, p. 81. Their analysis will not be presented here.

is stagnation. With a given stock of capital and a given cost and price structure, the system's operating rate cannot rise above the point at which the amount of surplus produced can find the necessary outlets. And this means chronic underutilization of available human and material resources. . . . Twist and turn as one will, there is no way to avoid the conclusion that monopoly capital is a self-contradictory system. . . . Left to itself . . . monopoly capitalism would sink deeper and deeper into a box of chronic depression."

But counteracting forces do exist. And they are all related to a desperate, ubiquitous effort to generate demand for the system's products. "The system has its own built-in selective mechanisms which have the most far-reaching consequences for every aspect of life in monopoly capitalist society."

The sales effort, with advertising as its leading form, plays a key role in stimulating demand. It does so in two quite distinct ways. First, it constitutes a resource-using expenditure "associated with higher employment of unproductive workers in advertising agencies, advertising media, and the like" and is thus income generating. In this it operates in a mode similar to government expenditures matched by tax revenues. Second, it creates demand for the products of the system. By inducing changes in fashion and setting new standards of status or norms of propriety it wages "a relentless war against saving and in favor of consumption" and, consequently, stimulates investment in plant and equipment which otherwise would not have taken place. "The unquestioned success of advertising in achieving these aims has greatly strengthened its role as a force counteracting monopoly capitalism's tendency to stagnation and at the same time marked it as the chief architect of the famous 'American Way of Life.' " [31]

Far from considering this contribution of the sales effort to the war against stagnation as salutary, Baran and Sweezy

[31] *Ibid.*, pp. 108, 111, 126, 128.

view its total impact on the human condition as utterly ne-farious. "An output the volume and composition of which are determined by the profit maximization policies of oligopolistic corporations neither corresponds to human needs nor costs the minimum possible amount of human toil and human suffer-ing." [32]

Not surprisingly, government expenditures constitute the main other form of surplus absorption. The capitalist class un-der conditions of monopoly capitalism is no longer hostile to an important and expanding role for government. Keynesian in spirit, it welcomes a large and increasing government budget, and (temporary) budgetary deficits as well. And this because it has come to recognize the need for government's interven-tion in maintaining the high and growing level of effective de-mand so necessary in absorbing the torrential output of the system. "The American ruling class, at any rate its leading echelon of managers of giant corporations, has learned these lessons through the rich experience of three decades of depres-sion, war, and Cold War. And its attitude toward taxation and government spending has undergone a fundamental change." Thus, for the authors, Keynes is the theorist par excellence of the monopoly stage of capitalism.

But "the big question . . . is not whether there will be more and more government spending, but on what. And here private interests come into their own as the controlling factor." Once again not surprisingly, the authors conclude that "it is of course in the area of defense purchases that most of the expansion has taken place. . . . This massive absorption of surplus in military preparations has been the key fact of post-war American economic history." For though in the abstract it may be possible to visualize the government as engaging in non-defense, effective demand generating expenditures, it is

[32] *Ibid.*, p. 139. I shall argue below that the authors' analysis of advertising — though plausible in its general form — ignores or understates the resource allo-cative implications of the selling effort of the modern corporate giants.

not likely that this lies within the realm of the possible in a capitalist society. In fact, "*given the power structure of United States monopoly capitalism, the increase of civilian spending had about reached its outer limits by 1939. The forces oppos-ing further expansion were too strong to be overcome.*" [33]

Thus, the absorption of surplus by government in the end amounts to absorption by militarism and imperialism. And this fits hand in glove the need of the ruling class to prevent on a global scale the spread of "communism"—the spread of the so-cialist form of society. "Here at last monopoly capitalism had seemingly found the answer to the 'on what' question: On what could government spend enough to keep the system from sinking into the mire of stagnation? On arms, more arms, and ever more arms. Yet it somehow has not worked out quite this way. The Cold War intensified; the military budget after a dip at the end of the Korean War, resumed its upward trend. But a sort of creeping stagnation set in all the same. . . . The fate-ful question 'on what' to which monopoly capitalism can find no answer in civilian spending has crept subversively into the military establishment itself. From all present indications there is no answer there either." [34]

[33] *Ibid.*, pp. 149, 151, 153, 161.
[34] *Ibid.*, pp. 213, 217.

Paternalistic Capitalism: The Economy

*A TECHNOCRATIC VIEW

J. K. Galbraith in his New Industrial State offers a technocratic interpretation of contemporary industrial society. The basic argument is rather simple. Modern technology imposes the necessity both for large size of the firm and for planning. This has consequences. "In the industrial enterprise, power rests with those who make decisions. In the mature enterprise, this power has passed, inevitably and irrevocably, from the individual to the group. That is because only the group has the information that decision requires. . . . Since technology and planning are what accord power to the technostructure,[1] the latter will have power wherever these are a feature of the productive process. Its power will not be peculiar to what in the cadenzas of ideology is called the free enterprise or capitalist system. If the intervention of private authority, in the form of owners, must be prevented in the private firm, so must the intervention of public authority in the public firm. . . . As a further consequence, puzzlement over capitalism without con-

[1] On pp. 82 and 163, Galbraith defines the technostructure as consisting of the "technicians, engineers, sales executives, scientists, designers and other specialists . . . who bring specialized knowledge or experience to group decision-making." All references are to the paperback Signet Book edition, 1968.

trol by the capitalist will be matched by puzzlement over socialism without control by society. . . . It seems likely that the Soviet resolution of the problem of authority in the industrial enterprise is not unlike that in the West—although no one can be precisely sure. Full social authority over the large enterprise is proclaimed. Like that of the stockholder and the Board of Directors in the United States, it is celebrated in all public ritual. The people and Party are paramount. But in practice large and increasing autonomy is accorded to the enterprise." [2]

Galbraith's fundamental thesis implies that capitalism and socialism are just ideological gibberish. However, notwithstanding this intended global applicability of the model of industrial society, Galbraith limits his analysis to the socioeconomic phenomena of contemporary American society. His attitude toward the system is that of a man who is at once a critic and an apologist. He is a critic insofar as he points up the failure of the system to respond to the needs and aspirations of modern man, especially to man in an affluent society. He is an apologist insofar as the emerging total view yields a more or less idealized, benign, and optimistic version of the actual state of affairs.

At the heart of the industrial system is the modern corporate conglomerate. This type of firm is not only gigantic, it is highly diversified. It does not sell a product or a service, nor does it operate primarily in one market. Indeed, its only at-

[2] Pp. 109–110, 118.

tribute is that it is an organization commanding an indefinable, and changing, production complex. Galbraith offers a historical justification for its size and structure. "It is clear, first of all, that industrial planning is in unabashed alliance with size. . . . Size is the general servant of technology, not the special servant of profits. . . . The enemy of the market is not ideology but the engineer. . . . The modern large corporation and the modern apparatus of socialist planning are variant accommodations to the same need." [3] The imperatives of modern technology impose upon us industrial planning, which, in turn, imposes large size and the suppression of the market. This is how the argument goes. It carries persuasion, but it will not do for the justification Galbraith intended it to be.

Surely, all but the pathologically romantic understand that modern technology imposes the need for industrial planning, as it does the need for large size. Are we to conclude from this, however, that the size *and* structure of the modern giants of American business are an expression of an inevitable historical necessity that arises from the imperatives of modern technology and industrial planning? My answer is an unqualified No! It ought to be clear that what Galbraith's argument requires for acceptance is much more than he offers. It is clearly not enough to argue, in general terms, that modern technology and industrial planning impose the need for some undefined "large" size and a "diversified" internal structure on the contemporary firm. It is essential, indeed mandatory, for his case to establish that the *particular* order of magnitude and the *particular* pattern of diversification of internal structure which characterizes the contemporary corporate conglomerate in the United States reflect the imperatives of modern technology and industrial planning.

We must look closely into Galbraith's argument. According to Galbraith, modern technology is characterized by the fol-

[3] *The New Industrial State*, pp. 42–44.

lowing features: lengthening of the production period; increase in the value of capital committed to the operation; lessened transferability of committed resources; greater reliance on specialized, organized knowledge; and greater emphasis on organization and coordination. These five technological, technical, and organizational features have as a consequence the necessity for planning. But that much abused term, *planning*, has yet to be defined.

Planning is rational behavior in a temporal context. Obviously it presupposes the existence of a planner, a decision-maker engaged in rational or systematic temporal search or pursuit of an acceptable or optimal state of affairs. Thus, to argue that the modern corporate giant engages in planning is to argue no more than that it behaves in a rational manner. And surely, it would not be necessary to invoke modern technology in order to establish the necessity for planning in the modern industrial unit. Clearly, Galbraith must have something else in mind than just that the large modern corporation acts rationally.

He does. His main point is that the firm has superseded the market or is in the process of doing so. "If the market is unreliable it [the firm] will not know these things [prices and costs]. Hence it cannot plan. If, with advancing technology and associated specialization, the market becomes increasingly unreliable, industrial planning will become increasingly impossible unless the market also gives way to planning. Much of what the firm regards as planning consists in minimizing or getting rid of market influences. . . . There are three ways of doing this: (1) The market can be superseded. (2) It can be controlled by sellers or buyers. (3) It can be suspended for definite or indefinite periods by contract between the parties to sale and purchase. All of these strategies are familiar features of the industrial system." [4] For the economist, "mini-

⁴ *Ibid.*, pp. 37–38.

mizing or getting rid of market influences" normally means simply acquiring monopoly power. Thus, the effort to reduce the unreliability of the market—to build up defensive and striking capabilities vis-à-vis competitors, to be free of the whim of the market—is understood by economists as behavior that flows naturally from the dynamics of market sharing in oligopolistic markets. Technology has only this to do with the problem: it explains in part (but only in part) the large size of the modern industrial unit and thus, indirectly, provides a partial explanation for the fact that markets are oligopolistic.

Are we entitled to conclude that Galbraith's planning is either no more than rational behavior in a temporal context pursued by firms whose size is necessarily large owing to technological advance, or no more than monopoly power–seeking behavior of oligopolists, a mere consequence of the dynamics of market sharing? I think not. Galbraith has more than this in mind. "The most obvious requirement of effective planning is large size. This, we have seen, allows the firm to accept market uncertainty where it cannot be eliminated; to eliminate markets in which it buys and it sells; and it is very nearly indispensable for participation in that part of the economy, characterized by exacting technology and comprehensive planning, where the only buyer is the Federal Government. . . . Nothing so characterizes the industrial system as the scale of the modern corporate enterprise. In 1962 the five largest industrial corporations in the United States, with combined assets in excess of $36 billion, possessed over 12 per cent of all assets used in manufacturing. The fifty largest corporations had over a third of all manufacturing assets. The 500 largest had well over two-thirds. Corporations with assets in excess of $10,000,000, some 2,000 in all, accounted for about 80 per cent of all the resources used in manufacturing in the United States. . . . Planning is a function that is associated in most minds with the state. If the corporation is the basic planning unit, it is appropriate that the scale of operations of the largest should approximate those of government. This they do. In 1965, three industrial corporations, General Motors, Standard Oil of New Jersey, and Ford Motor Company, had more gross income than all the farms in the country. The income of General Motors, of $20.7 billion, about equals that of the three million smallest farms in the country—around 90 per cent of all farms. The gross revenues of each of the three corporations just mentioned far exceed those of any single state. The revenues of General Motors in 1963 were fifty times those of Nevada, eight times those of New York and slightly less than one-fifth those of the Federal Government. . . . *The size of General Motors is in the service not of monopoly or the economies of scale but of planning. And for this planning—control of supply, control of demand, provision of capital, minimization of risk—there is no clear upper limit to the desirable size. It could be that the bigger the better.*" [5]

What Galbraith has in mind here is that the large private firm, the corporate giant, has achieved its monstrous size in order effectively to privatize a social process. Planning has come to capitalism—but it is not social planning. It is planning by the private managerial elite. Thus, the behavior of the large corporation in contemporary capitalism is not a direct consequence of the objective requirements of modern technology as Galbraith elsewhere obliquely suggests. Rather, it is a direct consequence of the structure, the institutions, and the overall value system of the contemporary capitalist society, and in the last analysis, of the goal system of the industrial firm. Thus, from a social point of view the acceptance or not of the expanding control by the modern corporate conglomerate over the social and economic process cannot be taken as historical necessity, a neutral concomitant of technological advance. It

[5] *Ibid.*, pp. 85–88. The emphasis is mine.

has to be judged on its own merits and in the light of the goals it serves.

* * * * *

Galbraith has much to say in relation to the goals of the industrial system and its framework, the industrial state. And this relates intimately to his views concerning the new ruling class, the technostructure, as he calls it. He makes the following propositions.

First, internal financing has made the industrial firm independent from outside sources of supply. "It no longer faces the risks of the market. It concedes no authority to outsiders. It has full control over its own expansion and over decisions between products, plants, and processes" (p. 50).

Second, "in the last three decades there has been steady accumulation of evidence on the shift of power from owners to managers within the modern large corporation. The power of the stockholders . . . has seemed increasingly tenuous" (p. 61).

Third, it is not, however, the managers alone that constitute the controlling force in the modern corporation. Control is in the hands of the technostructure. This is defined as "all who participate in group decision-making . . . all who bring specialized knowledge or experience to group decision-making" (p. 82). They are none other than the "technicians, engineers, sales executives, scientists, designers and other specialists" (p. 163).

Fourth, "power goes to the factor (of production) which is hardest to obtain or hardest to replace. In precise language it adheres to the one that has the greatest inelasticity of supply at the margin. This inelasticity may be the result of a natural shortage, or an effective control over supply by some human agency, or both. . . . One should expect, from past experience, to find a new shift of power in the industrial enterprise, this one from capital to organized intelligence. And one would expect that this shift would be reflected in the development of power in the society at large. . . . Power has, in fact, passed to what anyone in search of novelty might be justified in calling a new factor of production. This is the association of men of diverse technical knowledge, experience or other talent which modern industrial technology and planning require. It extends from the leadership of the modern industrial enterprise down to just short of the labor force" (pp. 67, 68, 69).

Fifth, "the technostructure does not supply capital, but specialized talent and organization. There is, a priori, no reason to believe that it will maximize the return to capital. More plausibly it will maximize its success as an organization" (p. 132).

Furthermore, "Power in economic life has over time passed from its ancient association with land to association with capital and then on, in recent times, to the composite of knowledge and skills which comprises the technostructure. Reflecting the symmetry that so conveniently characterizes reality, there have been associated shifts in the motivations to which men respond. Compulsion has an ancient association with land. Pecuniary motivation had a similar association with capital. Identification and adaptation are associated with the technostructure" (p. 150).

Sixth, "a secure level of earnings and a maximum rate of growth consistent with the provision of revenues for the requisite investment are the prime goals of the technostructure. Technological virtuosity and a rising dividend rate are sec-

71

ondary in the sense that they must not interfere with the two first-mentioned objectives" (p. 186).

Seventh, there is a carry-over from the goals of the techno-structure to generally accepted social goals. "No other social goal is more strongly avowed than economic growth. No other test of social success has such nearly unanimous acceptance as the annual increase in the Gross National Product" (p. 183).

Galbraith's points form a unified structure. Each of them has some factual basis. But the edifice as a whole is not plausible. Surely, its intended implications are not.

That internal financing is a major contributor to the growth of the modern corporate giant no one can deny. Agreement can provisionally[6] be obtained also on the relative independence of the management of the modern corporate firm from its stockholders, provided this independence is properly interpreted. I would suggest the following interpretation. The managerial elite is independent from the stockholders only in the sense that it designs and executes corporate strategies without reference to the stockholders' views. But these strategies are evolved in the context of norms which reflect the basic structure of power in capitalist society. The managerial elite in such a society is but the leading echelon of the Establishment,[7] an Establishment that, broadly speaking, identifies

[6] Provisionally, for we should not neglect the possibly important role of financial institutions in their stockholding capacity.

[7] The term *Establishment* is defined and discussed in the next chapter. The managerial elite, while being the leading echelon of the Establishment, is in a deeper sense the key mediating instrumentality of the property-owning class.

itself with the capitalist order and thus, of necessity, with the general interests of the property-owning class. On the assumption that the stockholders have ceased exercising operational control over the corporation, the managerial-capitalist elite becomes the focal source of control—indeed, almost identified with control. Galbraith's attempt, however, to substitute the technostructure for the mangerial-capitalist elite as the focus of power over the industrial firm is most certainly open to question. Surely, in the corporate Establishment, which is no more and no less than the corporation-controlling coalition, other groups beyond the management may well participate. Their role in it, their importance, depends undoubtedly on their relative scarcity, on the ease with which they may be replaced, on their ability because of their position in the process to interfere with and disrupt it. Thus, the techno-structure—exclusive of management proper—does have potential bargaining power, a power which potentially is superior to that of the labor union. But for their power to be more than a potential, they must develop an organizational co-hesiveness, an esprit de corps, a clear and autonomous concept of what they want as a group. Without these conditions, the members of Galbraith's technostructure have access to the Establishment on terms which are acceptable to the prepotent power in the Establishment—namely, the managerial elite. They become tamed and assimilated into the corporate Establishment, not as a new guiding force, but as a tool of the managerial elite. A process not too dissimilar to this has been characteristic of the labor unions. As Galbraith himself puts it in discussing the ministerial union, "the industrial system has now largely encompassed the labor movement. It has dissolved some of its important functions; it has greatly narrowed its area of action; and it has bent its residual operations very largely to its own needs. Since World War II, the acceptance of the union by the industrial firm and the emergence thereafter of an era of comparatively peaceful industrial relations have been hailed as the final triumph of trade unionism. On closer examination it is seen to reveal many of the features of Jonah's triumph over the whale."[8] This is exactly what I argue for Galbraith's technostructure—that its alleged ascent to power displays the features of Jonah's triumph over the whale. Thus, the members of the technostructure achieve no group power, as do the managers, but their values and methods are grist for the power that has been pre-empted by the managers. Oriented toward a technocratic, value-free approach and emphasizing, as they do, problem-solving techniques, they are more or less the willing servants of the managerial elite.

Is all this a haggling over labels? I think not. Let us return to Galbraith. "The managerial revolution as distinct from that of the technostructure is accepted. So long as earnings are above a certain minimum it would also be widely agreed that the management has little to fear from the stockholders. Yet it is for these stockholders, remote, powerless, and unknown, that management seeks to maximize profits. Management does not go out ruthlessly to reward itself—a sound management is expected to exercise restraint. Already at this stage, in the accepted view of the corporation, profit maximization involves a substantial contradiction. Those in charge forego personal reward to enhance it for others."[9]

But Galbraith is clearly wrong here. The managers, were they to pursue a policy of profit maximization for their firm, would not necessarily be enhancing the stockholders' personal reward. For, on his premises, the dividend policy of the management is tailor-made to the needs of the firm. If this be so, it might be argued that profit maximization does not have much to do with the stockholders' reward. But this would not imply that a profit-maximization policy is not attractive to

[8] *The New Industrial State*, p. 290.
[9] *Ibid.*, p. 126.

the managers, for—again on Galbraith's premises—the reinvestment of profits aggrandizes the firm, and the firm in every
meaningful sense *belongs* to the managers. The corporate form
substituted private-collective control for personal control over
capital. The separating of ownership from control, the passing
of control over the corporation to the managerial elite, substituted managerial-collective control for stockholder-collective
control over capital. In my opinion the change is *not* fundamental with respect to the motivation of a firm's behavior.
After all, even the capitalist-entrepreneur of old was not assumed to be maximizing profits in order to enhance his personal consumption. The concept of capital accumulation, of
reinvestment, of an expansionist dynamic, is part of the definition of capitalism. If the capitalist-entrepreneur of old was not
supposed to maximize profit in the interest of his personal consumption, why should we be surprised if we discover that the
manager-capitalist is playing out a social role which may well
call for maximizing profits. A successful performance carries
with it social rewards which include but are not coincident with
pecuniary rewards.

But there is something much more obviously dissonant in
Galbraith's argument. He posits, first, that the financing of
growth of the modern industrial firm is carried out from internal resources, and observes, second, that it is the very firms
which rely on internal financing that have achieved an astronomical size. It follows that their profits have been adequate
to the task—that they too have been astronomical. Is this an
accident? Even if we assume that growth is the primary objective and that profits are the means to its achievement, they
have to be earned.

This much on Galbraith's premises. The fact of the matter
is, however, that he overstates the case of internal financing,
of the independence of the modern giant firm from the
goings-on in the capital market. For though internally gen-

erated funds may well be the major source of financing for the modern giant corporation, this does *not* mean that the corporation's activities are carried out in disregard of their impact on the capital market. At the margin, the cost and the availability of funds from external sources do influence both the magnitude and the composition of internal investment projects. Furthermore, we cannot ignore the fact that the large U.S. firm has grown relatively more by means of mergers and acquisitions than through internal investment. Since most such external acquisitions are financed through an exchange of securities, the prices at which the capital markets value these securities play a very important role in determining the rate of a firm's growth. It follows that the conventional thesis—that firms maximize profits—is much nearer the truth than Galbraith is willing to admit because, logically, this seems to be the case either on his assumptions or on the conventional assumptions.

The modern corporation, in the process of privatizing the social process of planning, has reversed the sequence of control over the economic process. This is well brought out by Galbraith's argument. His "revised sequence" is at the heart of this issue. "In virtually all economic analysis . . . the initiative is assumed to lie with the consumer. . . . The flow of instruction is in one direction—from the individual to the market to the producer. . . . This is called consumer sovereignty. . . . We have seen that this sequence does not hold. . . . The mature corporation has readily at hand the means for controlling the prices at which it sells as well as those at which it buys. Similarly, it has means for managing what the consumer buys at the price it controls." [10]

The management of demand which assures that what is produced will also be bought, at controlled prices, is an essential attribute of the new system. This large-scale, expert manipulation of the public's values raises some fundamental and damaging questions about the productivity and the efficiency of the system. As Marcuse puts it, "We are again confronted with one of the most vexing aspects of advanced industrial civilization, the rational character of its irrationality. Its productivity and efficiency, its capacity to increase and spread comforts, to turn wants into needs, and destruction into construction, the extent to which this civilization transforms the object world into an extension of man's mind and body makes the very notion of alienation questionable. The people recognize themselves in their commodities; they find their soul in their automobile, hi-fi set, split-level home, kitchen equipment. The very mechanism which ties the individual to his society has changed, and social control is anchored in the new needs which it has produced." [11]

The machine no longer serves man, but man the machine. Technological change that held the hope of man's freedom has imposed upon him a much subtler but more tenacious form of servitude.

To put the matter more precisely, the modern industrial system serves ends which to a large extent are shaped by its own requirements. Ultimate ends are no longer independent of the profit-through-growth or growth-through-profit requirements of the modern corporate giant. This no longer raises only questions of efficiency, but the much more basic question of effectiveness. Had we been able to define ultimate

[10] *Ibid.*, pp. 221–222.
[11] Herbert Marcuse, *One Dimensional Man* (Boston: Beacon Press, 1964), p. 9.

ends—the ends of the consumer and the state—independently of the influences of the industrial system, we would have been in a position to establish almost certainly that these ends are *not* served by it. The fact is that we cannot even do that. The economic process has become *irrational* de profundis.

This undoubtedly is the gist of Galbraith's emphasis on planning by the technostructure. Technically, but only technically, the market mechanism still allocates resources to uses. But consumer sovereignty is no longer present. The system has become *paternalistic*. This can be understood best by reference to an example of a planned economy—where the planning authority relies on the market mechanism to allocate resources, but where, also, it substitutes its own preferences for those of the consumer. This can be achieved by the imposition of an appropriately designed (and rather elaborate) system of indirect taxes.[12] Suppose now that instead of a public planning authority we are dealing with a huge corporation in private hands that owns (directly or indirectly) all productive units in the economy. Such a super-monopolist has no less power over the economy's price structure than the tax authority. Thus, it is proper to think of this super-monopolist as both able and willing to allocate resources to uses in a manner entirely analogous to that employed by a public planning authority. Except, of course, that in the case of the super-monopolist the allocation of resources is intended to suit his own preferences. And in the context of a capitalist society, these preferences would necessarily be a reflection of the super-monopolist's "systematic temporal search for highest practicable profits."

This example of the super-monopolist who employs the market mechanism to allocate resources in a manner that suits his own ends is suggestive—but only suggestive—of what takes place in the contemporary, advanced capitalist economy.

[12] See, for instance, Hansen, *Lectures in Economic Theory*, pp. 86–87.

I am certainly not suggesting that the corporate establishment behaves as if it were one huge firm. But the interlocking networks of industrial command, the size of the modern corporate giants, and the basically cooperative strategies pursued by them clearly make possible a more or less extensive employment of this type of planning technique. To the extent that they succeed, they may be said to supersede the market. Naturally, in an oligopolistic economy, this collective imposition of the price-structure that reflects the internal needs of the industrial system requires generous employment of selling expenditures (the sales effort). The level and structure of selling expenditures is interdependent with the intended price structure, since the oligopolists must be in a position to dispose of their planned output at the planned prices.

It should be clear, of course, that the level (as against the structure) of the selling expenditures (to be undertaken by the corporate world) required to dispose of a given output at the planned prices depends on the fiscal and monetary policies pursued by the public sector. It depends also on world income—and its rate of growth—especially as its concerns the country's key "trading partners." Thus relevant to the corporate world's decisions in any one country are also the policies pursued by the governments of that country's key trading partners.

With this interpretation, Galbraith's argument—that in the modern industrial state planning is superseding the market—has an important and revealing meaning. Contemporary capitalism, in these terms, takes on a definite paternalistic flavor.[13] It becomes paternalistic capitalism. In my view this paternalistic character of contemporary capitalism is an excellent working hypothesis for understanding the overall behavior of the system.

What is remarkable is that this valuable insight into the

[13] "What is good for General Motors is good for the country."

workings of contemporary capitalism is shared by so few. Consider, for instance, Baran and Sweezy's position: "Overall, monopoly capitalism is as unplanned as its competitive predecessor. The big corporations relate to each other, to consumers, to labor, to smaller business primarily through the market. The way the system works is still the unintended outcome of the self-regarding actions of the numerous units that compose it. And since market relations are essentially price relations, the study of monopoly capitalism, like that of competitive capitalism, must begin with the workings of the price mechanism."[14] I cannot agree with this view. The markets exist in monopoly capitalism as they did in competitive capitalism, but they perform quite different functions. Paternalistic, capitalist planning has replaced or is replacing consumer sovereignty.

*PROLEGOMENA TO AN ECONOMIC THEORY OF PATERNALISTIC CAPITALISM

I have made it quite clear that, in my view, the orthodox theory concerning the behavior of the contemporary capitalist economy is not even a caricature of the true state of affairs. Is there an alternative theory—a comprehensive, coherent, and plausible formulation ready to take its place? I think not. However, many valuable insights about the proper direction that a theory construction effort should follow are available. As we have seen, they are contained in Neo-Marxist literature and in the work of some liberal economists, as exemplified by Galbraith's contribution. In this section, I shall present some further thoughts intended to contribute to this effort of building a new, articulate view of contemporary paternalistic capitalism.[15]

[14] Monopoly Capital, p. 53.
[15] The comments in this section are limited to the behavior of the business system in the capitalist metropolis. The argument is extended and rounded out in the chapter "The New Mercantilism."

* * * * *

Galbraith's "revised sequence," though fundamentally valid, requires some sharpening of focus. The proper framework for analysis of the behavior of the modern giant corporation is to be sought in the conceptual apparatus of games of strategy. This in no sense contradicts the view that the contemporary large firm engages in "a systematic temporal search for highest practicable profits." Rather, it places this search in the appropriate decision framework. For verification, let us turn to a member of the corporate elite, Donald J. Smalter, who conducted a study of Department of Defense practices and activities: "My company has no business whatsoever with the Department of Defense, so my interest related strictly to the observation of DOD methodologies, their analytical techniques, and the usefulness of these to the management of large corporations. . . . What McNamara instituted was planning by missions. . . . Key missions were identified, e.g., a nuclear retaliation mission, a 'hot-spot response' mission requiring high-capacity airlift of police type forces, etc. In a complete 5-year plan, strategic elements and their supporting expenditures were assembled in what has been popularly termed 'mission program-packages.' . . . What lessons can be gained from this? Permit me to try to clarify the fundamental concept of mission planning. The top management job might be described as allocating limited resources, for select mission purposes in the dimension of *time*. . . . Although International Minerals and Chemical Corporation has been essentially a mining company, even before we instituted market-mission planning we had significantly progressed toward a greater emphasis on market orientation. . . . Our thoughts must give dominant attention to *market* challenges. Corporations possess certain 'internal' opportunities . . . but the majority of our opportunities will exist 'externally.' . . . Many commercial development authors profess that a product-line should establish its own 'ecological niche' in the market place. . . . What proprietary directions for growth are desirable? What pioneering aims are sought? . . . Next, it is desirable to understand your basic *position* through conduct of an audit. What's your participation in the industry structure? Where are the greatest profit margins? What's the product life-cycle status of each product? What market share do the products possess? . . . Next the relevant *environment* must be examined. It is vital that management look outward to be aware of the rapidly changing environment in which the company exists. What is the market demand outlook for the product-line? What are the present distribution channels, and the possibilities of advantageously altering those channels? What impact is changing technology going to have? We must then ascertain our relative position in this ever-changing environment. What are the problems, needs, threats and opportunities? What are the most important challenges? Next we must establish what our *momentum* is going to achieve. What are the prospects anticipated? Are we going to have continued growth? Or do we have some major product that will become obsolete?" [16]

This quotation gives the flavor of top-management thinking on the proper framework of corporate decision-making. The key words are *position, environment, momentum*. The corporate manager views the future as a succession of expected positions in expected environments. Each position in the sequence, once attained, limits the historically possible positions in the unfolding future. This anticipated historical nexus among successive positions in successive environments is of the essence. The decisions of a corporate manager *today* determine in which subset of the set of all expected (possible)

---

[16] "The Influence of Department of Defense Practices on Corporate Planning," *Management Technology*, Vol. 4, No. 2, December 1964, pp. 115–138.

trajectories he will find himself. At each point in time a
position—given the *environment*—is associated with some
profit. The sequence of profits, the profits trajectory, is at
once the objective and the condition that guarantees the feasibility of the corresponding trajectory of positions. Thus, the
corporate manager views his decision problem at any one time
as a problem of choosing among self-sustaining sequences or
trajectories of positions. And the norm for his choice is profits.
That is to say, he will choose that sequence which is *profit
dominant.*[17]

Now, one aspect of the position of the corporate enterprise
at any one time is the product mix it puts on the market. This
product mix is a reflection at once of the technology employed
by the firm, of its asset structure, and of its relative position
in the complex of markets in which it operates. It is a reflection, also, of the course it has chosen, the trajectory it has
chosen to ride. Given consumer preferences and aggregate
income and its distribution, this product mix will be removed
from the market for some given combination of sales effort
and product prices. The sales effort—which includes advertising, but covers the whole range of marketing strategy—
shifts consumer tastes in the desired direction (affecting, as
well, the propensity to consume out of income). The price
structure of the product mix is so designed as to dispose of
the firm's output, given consumer tastes as shaped by the
sales effort. The prices set by the firm for a given product mix
placed on the market determine its gross revenue, and the
sales effort is a component of its total cost. It is to be expected

[17] A technically precise formulation of this decision problem lies beyond the
scope of this book. It should be stressed that the argument here is based on the
not altogether valid assumption that the corporation serves its own interests,
rather than, those of a structured external interest group. It is not difficult, however, to substitute for the "industrial" profits, the profits, say, of a financial institution that succeeds in dominating or influencing corporate policies. However,
since financial institutions have interests far broader in scope than those of any
one corporation, this could have significant implications for the mode of behavior of any one of the controlled or influenced corporate units.

that the combination of sales effort and product prices will be selected in such a way as to maximize profits—but this maximization is constrained by the fact that the firm is placing on the market a predetermined product mix. And this would seem to contradict the notion that the overall strategy of the firm is profit-maximizing. Why, in other words, should the firm constrain its search for maximum profits by committing itself to a particular product mix? But we already have the answer to this riddle. It will do so because it is not intent upon maximizing profits at a particular time, independently of the impact of such maximization on future profits. Since its position (say, in the market complex) at any one time is a historical link with its position in the future, a suboptimum situation today may well be a necessary condition for riding the optimum trajectory. And since every day becomes "today," there is no reason to expect that the product mix placed on the market at any one time is profit maximizing at that time. And this is due, of course, to the fact that the process is evolutionary de profundis.

The price structure selected by the corporate management is intended to dispose of its product mix, given the level and structure of its sales effort. This market price structure, which may be characterized as external, may, normally, be expected to deviate from the production realities which are internal to the firm. Thus, the rate at which any of the components of the product mix may be substituted for another component in production need have no relation to their relative market prices. In other words, if the firm were to institute internal signalling devices—that is, internal planning prices—they should be expected to deviate from market prices. This is analogous to the deviation of prices net of indirect taxes from prices inclusive of indirect taxes. And it is in this sense that I claim a similarity between the behavior of the modern corporate giant with that of a public planning authority that relies on the market to allocate resources according to its own preferences by employing an appropriately designed system of indirect taxes.

Of course, the modern corporate firm is not likely to tinker with prices too much or too often. Prices represent its stockpile of "nuclear weapons." This explains their "stickiness," and it explains, as well, the fact that price changes occur in the context of industry-wide (tacit) decisions initiated by the price leader. Thus, prices in oligopolistic markets are characteristically determined on an industry-wide basis, not on a firm-by-firm basis. In respect to market prices, the planning unit is the industry, not the firm. To achieve its objectives, the individual firm is forced to rely much more on its overall marketing strategy, its sales effort, rather than on pricing. But the price leader, if he is to retain his position, must, in setting the industry's price structure, attempt to take account of the rest of the industry's views of what is an appropriate structure.

It is not an exaggeration to argue that the corporate Establishment plans the product mix made available to consumers over time on the basis of its own long-term growth-through-profit and profit-through-growth requirements. The sovereign is not the consumer but the corporate Establishment. This planning is, of course, highly decentralized. Prices are set by industry-wide instrumentalities or institutions. The level and structure of the sales effort and the rate of introduction of new products and of new technologies are determined at the firm level—but within a set of customs which, generally speaking, take form and become legitimate at the industry-wide level.

Thus, at the industry level the appropriate instrumentalities and social processes seem to have emerged for more or less effective, albeit decentralized planning. And since each giant corporate firm participates simultaneously in a large set of markets and is a member, therefore, of many industries at once, the industrial sector's behavior may be said to converge to a process which is best understood and interpreted as a planned process. This process is surely reinforced by the not insignificant role played by financial institutions whose influence extends throughout the economy. Indeed, it is conceivably increasingly important in the implementation of the economy-wide capitalist planning process. To the extent, of course, that this situation obtains, planning will tend to serve the ends (profits) of the financial institutions—that is, the profitability of the system as a whole rather than that of individual corporations.

It may be countered that the dynamics of market sharing—involving as it does the continuous introduction of cost-reducing technologies and of new products and gadgets, and visibly aggressive styles of selling strategies—suggests anything but the presence of a planned process, so far as it concerns the behavior of the industrial sector as a whole. But there is nothing inconsistent in principle in positing the presence of a planned process which incorporates some lively competition —in particular channels and within a set of legitimated behavioral patterns. For indeed, the behavior of the contemporary giant corporate enterprise, *taken by itself*, is best understood and interpreted as a decentralized planning process. The competition among divisions and branches of one and the same enterprise may be as ferocious as that between two distinct corporate complexes, but no one would be prepared to argue that interbranch competition is not a component of the overall consciously designed strategy of the corporate enterprise. And though at the level of the industrial sector the overall strategy is not necessarily consciously designed, the simultaneous presence of each giant corporate enterprise in many markets and industries, interlocking directorates, the strictures imposed upon corporate growth and behavior by financial institutions, and the sharing by the corporate managers in the values, beliefs, and activities of the social elite to which they consciously belong undoubtedly provide the necessary instrumentalities and institutions for the emergence of an overall behavior pattern of the industrial sector which may legitimately be considered as an instance of planning.

Organized labor, a junior partner in the ruling coalition, plays no doubt a significant role in the price-setting process. The dynamics of the power game between corporate management and union management have direct and immediate implications on the rate of inflation—and through it on the distribution of the wage share (and unemployment) among the members of the working class, as well as on the distribution of profits or "surplus" among the members of the corporate world. The state's manipulation of the flow of aggregate demand through monetary and fiscal policies must be consistent at once with the overall growth goals of the corporate Establishment and with its income-distributive requirements. Thus, in paternalistic capitalism the overall economic process may be viewed as a super-game with main players the corporate managers, labor union leadership and the key instrumentalities of the state apparat. If we take into account that the economy is not "closed" to the rest of the world, the country's key "trading partners" must also be included in the set of players.[18]

I argue in the following chapter that in paternalistic capitalism the main players who participate in the super-game are members of the coalition of vested interests that gives form to the Establishment, an Establishment dominated by the corporate elite. Thus the rules that define the super-game— a game that effectuates the economy-wide planning process in paternalistic capitalism—necessarily reflect the values, goals, and aspirations of the Establishment.

[18] This type of planning process is an instance of polycentric planning. The concept is discussed in the last chapter. Thus, if we must attach a label to modern capitalistic planning, that label would include the terms paternalistic and polycentric.

Of course, it is an error to view the Establishment as being monolithic and immutable. In any particular instance, within the framework of the all-inclusive, grand coalition that defines the Establishment, particular, special-purpose, short-term coalitions may take form and shape. The corporate managers are not united on every issue, nor are trade union leaders, state instrumentalities, or "trading partners." Where the internal contradictions in the Establishment exceed certain limits, the super-game may well break down. Indeed, there is good reason to believe that the internal contradictions of the system are both significant and progressively malignant. A good example at the international level is the havoc that resulted in the Western world as a result of Richard Nixon's camouflaged and punitive devaluation of the dollar in 1971.

In the measure that the successive outcomes of this evolving super-game fall within a framework of "solutions" more or less consistent with the requirements of the prevailing social order and with the values of the Establishment—in that measure the economic process may legitimately be viewed as a planned process. What is more, instances where it cannot be so viewed are necessarily instances of crisis, not only in respect to the course of the economy, but also in respect to the internal equilibrium of the Establishment. Cases in point are protracted strikes in key industries, serious difficulties in the balance of payments, rates of inflation and unemployment that are considered threats to the global social equilibrium, and so on.

Failures of this type clearly are not planned. Nor, of course, is the underfulfillment of a Soviet quantitative plan. But no one would be prepared to argue that failure of a Soviet plan implies absence of planning. Rather, it implies either inadequate planning, or adverse developments in conditions beyond the planner's reach, or indeed internal contradictions in the social system's dynamics and conflict within the Establishment.

The Economy

To the extent that capitalist society is beset by deep-seated contradictions, to that extent the emerging pattern of decentralized capitalist planning is certain to run into rough seas. And the tendency, inevitably, will be toward centralization—centralization in the planning process that will go hand in hand with totalitarian reforms, and a bigger and more powerful State.

Paternalistic Capitalism: The State

*THE ROLE OF THE STATE
IN PATERNALISTIC CAPITALISM

For market capitalism, the State's role was limited to providing the legal framework for its operations as well as, of course, to assisting its expansion beyond the nation's shores in imperialistic adventures. Paternalistic capitalism expects much more from the State. To begin with, it relies on the social regulation of aggregate demand, since the modern corporations cannot guarantee through their actions that the flow of aggregate demand will be adequate to the task of removing from the market their planned output at the controlled prices. This burden falls upon the State, which through its fiscal policy and monetary management prevents a slump in aggregate demand. And since taxation is the chosen instrument for achieving this objective, the revenues of the State must be large enough in relation to national income to perform this role effectively. Thus, a "large" State is welcomed by the managerial-capitalist elite. But the expenditures side of the ledger must not be thought unimportant because a significant part of the corporate firm's costs may well be *socialized*—that is, they may be borne by the citizens. Education—especially education that is intended to

90

increase the supply of specialists needed by the modern corporation—becomes legitimately a State responsibility. The major technological breakthroughs, especially those that have to do with the space exploration and armaments, may also be assigned to the State, their cost being assumed by the citizens. As Galbraith puts it: "The State is strongly concerned with the stability of the economy. And with expansion and growth. And with education. And with technical and scientific advance. And, most notably, with the national defense. These are *the* national goals: they are sufficiently trite so that one has a reassuring sense of the obvious in articulating them. All have their counterpart in the needs and goals of the technostructure. It requires stability in demand for its planning. . . . It requires trained manpower. It needs government underwriting of research and development. Military and other technical procurement support its most developed form of planning. At each point the government has goals with which the technostructure can identify itself. Or, plausibly, these goals reflect adaptation of public goals to the goals of the technostructure."[1]

Thus, the State in paternalistic capitalism has become a cog in the process of private planning by the corporate establishment. Its domestic tasks call for the socialization of the research and development costs of private enterprise, the provision of an increasingly elaborate infrastructure, the control of aggregate demand, and the effectuation of industrial peace (that is, the development of a mechanism for settling industrial disputes without disruption of the economic process). Characteristically in paternalistic capitalism, areas crucial for community welfare are left to their fate—the city being a prime example.

But there is more. The modern contract system has led to the contracting out to the private sphere of a significant part of the public domain. "Under the pressures of the Second

[1] *The New Industrial State*, p. 316.

World War, contracting procedures on aircraft, ordnance, and ammunition reverted to the cost-plus basis which had inspired . . . earlier scandals. Then a series of developments after the war produced the current unprecedented state of affairs. First, as part of a movement heralded as a return to 'free enterprise,' plants, factories and facilities built by the government during the war were either sold to private corporations, usually at a fraction of their original cost, or were leased at nominal fees to contractors, to use for military contracts. This largely deprived the government of the performance 'yardstick' of its in-house facilities. Second, the Air Force was established as an independent military service. Naturally, it did not have the already built in-house capabilities of the other two services, so it hired out the entire process of designing, producing and even maintaining weapons systems, instead of presenting its own designs to contractors for production. This necessitated a cost-plus contractual basis, since no prearranged price could be fixed for so indeterminate a process. In addition, the Air Force's prime contracting corporations, now responsible for complete weapons systems, had to establish, in the words of one Congressional Report, 'procurement organizations and methods which proximate those of government.' These prime contractors were thus in a position to force subcontracting small companies out of business, acquire their proprietary information, make or break geographical regions and decide a host of other critical issues of national import, without even the quasi-democratic checks imposed on the federal bureaucracy. . . . Once established, prime systems contracting quickly spread to the other services. A losing battle with the Air Force for responsibility for missile program development taught the Army that its extensive in-house capabilities and technical independence were a distinct disadvantage. For in the political struggle over missile development, the Air Force's corporate prime contractors constituted a powerful lobby in Congress against which all the in-house expertise of the Army was of no avail. A quick learner when the future of its bureaucracy is at stake, the Army began to disband its in-house facilities and to surrender its jurisdictional and discretionary capacities to private industry and the latter's impressive political power. For any corporation in advanced technologies on the way up, prime contracting soon became the indispensable order of the day."[2]

Thus, not surprisingly, the modern giant corporation has come to exercise decisive influence over national defense and foreign policy because the most significant single customer of the industrial system in the contemporary United States is the Pentagon. "The government defense-industry nexus defies most of the rules of the free-enterprise economy. The essence of the free-enterprise system is competition, but 57.9 percent of all defense procurement is negotiated with a single contractor and only 11.5 percent through formal advertised competition. Under capitalist creed, the efficient survive, and those who can neither provide quality nor control their costs fall by the wayside. Defense industry . . . is shielded by the government from the harsher realities of the competitive system. It is relieved of the obligation to be efficient and is protected by the government from most of the normal risks of doing business for profit. . . . The defense contractor develops his new products and the market for them simultaneously, often in close, continuous association with the customer, the Department of Defense. Thus he can normally count on selling them."

But who holds the upper hand in the military goods sector? the sellers or the customer? the corporations or the Department of Defense? According to Barnet, "the ultimate power to distribute the $45 billion now spent annually on procurement resides in the Pentagon itself. . . . In the Department of Defense the leading defense contractors are regarded as sub-

[2] David Horowitz and Reese Erlich, "Big Brother as a Holding Company," *Ramparts*, Vol. 7, No. 8, November 30, 1968, pp. 42–52.

sidiaries that must be protected for the benefit of the whole system." [3] Of course, one cannot disagree with Barnet that the ultimate power lies with the Pentagon. But it does so only in relations with each of the contractors, taken separately. The overall behavior of the Pentagon, however, cannot be understood independently from the social order of which it is a part.

As a matter of fact, one could speculate that "the Department of Defense has become the closest thing to a *central planning* agency in American Society. It uses the military budget to stimulate economic growth, to put money into circulation in times of recession, to encourage the development of specific industries, and to assist in certain geographical areas." [4] *Thus, the Pentagon is emerging as a potential central planning Board of U.S. society.* Surely, the Department of the Treasury, the Federal Reserve Board, and the Council of Economic Advisers constitute significant complementary instrumentalities. But the Pentagon has the distinctive feature of playing a key and direct role in the resource-allocative process of the economy. A protracted war in Indochina and new, bigger Vietnams will move it definitively into the focus of the process, and will turn it into a dominant central planning agency. If, through extended war, the process reaches a mature stage, the U.S. economy will have taken on all the characteristics of a centrally planned economy. With a difference: the planning will be essentially in private (corporate) hands and it will have the flavor of a distinctly militarized society.

*THE STATE, THE ESTABLISHMENT, AND THE RULING CLASS

The increasingly dominant role of the State in contemporary society East or West is all too obvious to require extensive

[3] Richard J. Barnet, *The Economy of Death* (New York: Atheneum, 1970), pp. 112–113, 118, 120.
[4] *Ibid.*, pp. 122–123. The emphasis is mine.

comment. Our generation has witnessed the spectacular transformation that has led to the emergence of the modern state which reaches out to influence and control almost every aspect of the citizen's life. The fundamental propelling forces behind the expansionist dynamic of the State are not far to seek. They lie in the nature of social conflict among sectional interests, whether regional or functional, which find it necessary to be allied with or to occupy the seat of power in order to promote vested interests. And they lie also in the spectacular technological and organizational innovations which have placed at the disposal of the State power that no authority or group other than the State can challenge effectively. They lie, finally, in the state power–reinforcing character of the conflict among nations.

The word *state* has two connotations.[5] One of them refers to any organized society with a distinct government. This is the context which permits us to think of ourselves as belonging to a state, as being the State. The other connotation refers to the powerhouse, the *apparat* that exercises command. This apparat is a specialized organization performing a service which is best summed up by the word *command*. The members of this apparat wield power in varying degrees—a special kind of power, for it is viewed as being legitimate. That is, the commands of the State are obeyed by the citizens in part at least because they are considered legitimate, though certainly, the State's commands are also backed by compulsion, for every citizen is deeply aware of the overriding strength of the State's commands. Being a member of the organized society over which the State apparat exercises command, the citizen is inclined to view it as a *beneficent* instrumentality serving the common good, a goal considered by the citizen as superior to his own. This belief in the State's beneficence leads to iden-

[5] The argument in this section is an adaptation of "Democracy: Myth and Reality" in A. G. Papandreou, *Man's Freedom* (New York & London: Columbia University Press, 1970).

tification of the citizen with the State—a powerful motivation, which along with the belief in the legitimacy of the State's commands, and the ever-present knowledge of its capability to enforce them, accounts for the citizen's obedience. It accounts, in other words, for the citizen's willingness to accept the state's command as authoritative, his willingness to accept it as a communication guiding his actions.

Of the three motivations that underlie the citizen's obedience to the State's commands, the belief in their legitimacy is the hardest one to come to grips with because it has definite metaphysical or mythological connotations. It requires the construction of a myth. Historically, there have been two kinds of myths, both relying on the concept of sovereignty. In the one case, God is the supreme sovereign; in the other, society itself is. According to the myth of divine sovereignty, the State must perform in accordance with the dictates of God, whose representative on Earth is the Church. According to the myth of popular sovereignty, the State must perform in accordance with the dictates of the representatives of the people, parliament. In both instances, there is a conflict between trustor and trustee—between monarchy and Church in times past, between the executive and the legislature in modern times. Monarchy won over the Church in the Middle Ages, as in modern times the executive won over the legislature.

With the decline of the myth of divine sovereignty in modern times, and the substitution for it of the myth of popular sovereignty, there was born—practically at the same time—the concept of the nation. The nation, a product of the French Revolution, gave a new twist to the concept of sovereignty. For with the rise of the nation-state, popular sovereignty merged with national sovereignty; the legitimacy of the State's commands now derived from the fact that it became the mandatory of the nation; and its beneficence came to be judged in terms of its service to the goals of the nation.

* * * * *

So much for the myths that surround the concept of the State, especially the modern nation-state. Beyond the myths there are misunderstandings. The most common one is the confusion of two quite distinct entities, that of the *State* with the *Government*. "The point is by no means academic. For the treatment of one part of the state—usually the government— as the state itself introduces a major element of confusion in the discussion of the nature and incidence of state power; and that confusion can have large political consequences. Thus, if it is believed that the government is in fact the state, it may also be believed that the assumption of governmental power is equivalent to the acquisition of state power. Such a belief, resting as it does on vast assumptions about the nature of state power, is fraught with great risks. . . . To understand the nature of state power, it is necessary first of all to distinguish, and then to relate, the various elements which make up the state system. It is not very surprising that government and state should often appear as synonymous. For it is the government which speaks on the state's behalf. . . . The fact that the government does speak in the name of the state and is formally *invested* with state power, does not mean that it effectively *controls* that power. . . . A second element of the state . . . is the administrative one, which now extends far beyond the traditional bureaucracy of the state, and which encompasses a large variety of bodies, often related to particular ministerial departments, or enjoying a greater or lesser degree of autonomy—public corporations, central banks, regulatory commissions, etc.—and concerned with the management of the economic, social, cultural and other activities in which the state is now directly or indirectly involved. The extraordinary growth of this administrative and bureaucratic element in all societies

. . . and the relation of its leading members to the government and to society is also crucial to the determination of the role of the state. Formally, officialdom is at the service of the political executive, its obedient instrument, the tool of its will. In actual fact it is nothing of the kind. . . . As Professor Meynaud notes, 'the establishment of an absolute separation between the political and administrative sectors has never represented much more than a simple juridical fiction of which the ideological consequences are not negligible.' Some of these considerations apply to all other elements of the state system. They apply for instance to a third such element, namely the military, to which may . . . be added the para-military, security and police forces of the state, and which together form that branch of it mainly concerned with the 'management of violence.'" But beyond these three distinct expressions of the State, we have the judicial branch, subcentral government, and parliamentary assemblies. These institutions, taken together, make up the State. Their "interrelationship shapes the form of the state system. It is these institutions in which 'state power' lies, and it is through them that this power is wielded in its different manifestations by the people who occupy the leading positions in each of these institutions—presidents, prime ministers and their ministerial colleagues; high civil servants and other state administrators; top military men; judges of the higher courts; some at least of the leading members of parliamentary assemblies . . . and a long way behind, particularly in unitary states, the political and administrative leaders of sub-central units of the state. These are the people who constitute what may be described as the *state elite*."[6]

Who controls the State? The classical concept of representative democracy, according to which citizens are supposed to have equal power over political affairs through their elected

[6] Ralph Miliband, *The State in Capitalist Society* (New York: Basic Books, 1969), pp. 49, 50, 51, 54. The emphasis is mine.

representatives, is not even a caricature of the true state of affairs. For the members of the legislative assemblies do act neither as individuals, on the basis of their personal value system, nor as the mouthpieces of the electorate. They act, rather, as members of a *party*, a component of the political system which takes clear, definitive predominance over their personal views. The contemporary party is indeed a fundamental instrumentality for the exercise of power, not only because it is itself an organization aiming at access to the main focus of power, but also because it is a social mechanism for developing a modus vivendi, a particular form of peace among groups and organizations which are specifically interested in influencing it.

This modus vivendi is to be sought, generally speaking, in the context of the prevailing social order. If there exists only one party, as is the case with the Soviet Republics, then it becomes itself the focus of conflict over the working out of a grand compromise among a variety of influences present in society—always, of course, within the confines of the established social order. If there are just two parties, as is (was?) the case in the United States of America, exactly because the situation is duopolistic, slogans apart, both parties make an effort to achieve a workable national compromise, and thus their differences in practice turn out to be quite small. Naturally, there is an assumption behind this position, namely, that neither of the two parties challenges the established order in a fundamental way. If it happened that one of the two did so, the situation would be quite different. Indeed, we would then talk of a polarization of the political forces of the nation in question, and a deep conflict situation, latent or open, would be in the offing. Whenever three or more substantial parties are in existence, each party ceases the attempt to develop a grand compromise among the overall forces which are operative upon it. It selects those forces and influences which it wishes to respond to and develops its platform accordingly.

Under these circumstances, the formation of a government pre-supposes generally the formation of a coalition among parties and the corresponding formulation of an ad hoc minimum program representing the overlap of the programmatic positions of the parties participating in the coalition.

The emergence of the modern party in a dominant position in the political process has reversed the relationship between parliament and cabinet. Initially, the cabinet was viewed as a committee of the parliament—the parliament having thus concentrated in its hands both the legislative and the executive powers. With the emergence of the party and party discipline, the members of parliament, having increasingly assumed the more or less perfunctory role of adding up to a number that may or may not ensure a majority, can do no more than follow the dictates of the cabinet, which has the direct support of the party in power. Thus, the parliamentary committee of the party, as it is called today, often does nothing more than execute the orders of the executive, which has fused legislative and executive functions. Many important exceptions can be found to this interpretation of the relationship among parliament, cabinet, and party. Yet in substance it is correct.

Elections increasingly take the form of a plebiscite for or against a party and a program. With his vote the citizen delivers to a party both legislative and executive functions. He is a sovereign citizen for just that day, returning to his role as subject the moment after he has cast his ballot.

But even his vote is typically not the expression of his mature judgment, of his unfettered will. For political machines have taken on the role of delivering the vote to the candidate of their, not the citizen's choice, just as they have taken over the task of developing the image of the candidate and, to a large extent, his stands on public issues. What matters in the end is that the machine's candidate wins the seat.

The political machine is but an aspect of a vast network of

channels and mechanisms, formal and informal, which perform the role of conduit for the exercise of power by the syndicates of interest, the enclaves of power that vie for control over the powerhouse of the State. Political power, whether it runs in formal channels or outside them, is the power to influence directly or indirectly the State system—the cabinet, the parliamentary assembly, the bureaucracy, all the instrumentalities that make up the apparat of the State—in the process of making decisions which are appropriate to their specified function within the State.

Naturally, the relative importance of political power in any society depends directly on the relative importance of the State's functions in the overall socioeconomic processes of that society. Clearly, for instance, political power in a centrally planned economy is relatively more important in that society than is political power in a decentralized market economy. Thus, political power is merely an aspect of the power, independently of the concrete form it may take, to influence the vital socioeconomic processes of a society. And it is not, in general, possible to delineate sharply political power as distinct, say, from economic power, because the methods of influencing the State are intimately related to the overall social process. Controlling or affecting the process of recruitment of the state elite is undoubtedly of paramount importance for the effective, long-term exercise of political power. Yet this recruitment process merges imperceptibly into the overall social process. Equally important is the creation of the appropriate ideological climate. Effective indoctrination of the populace and development of the proper creed may well constitute the most fundamental conditions for the legitimation of a particular distribution of political power. Here again, however, we are dealing with social processes that are much more encompassing than the political process.

PATERNALISTIC CAPITALISM

* * * * *

The pressure groups, power enclaves, or power oligopolies that exercise influence over the vital social, economic, political processes in the modern, industrially advanced, capitalist society fall into two basic categories. There is, first, the state elite that speaks in the name of society at large or in the name of the nation, identifying itself with the general interest. Clearly, this elite claims for itself the official monopoly of "neutrality" vis-à-vis the various sectional interests. The political elite is, in general, identified with sectional interests—for instance, as party leader, a prime minister is permitted a wide range of activities that are inconsistent with his role as prime minister. Fictions apart, the state elite must be viewed as a power enclave, or rather as a system of power enclaves, capable of exercising the most substantial and direct influence over the processes within the purview of the State. The second category consists of the spokesmen for structured, visible, or surfaced sectional interests. These interests range all the way from the large corporation, to the industrial association, the chamber of commerce, the trade union, the agricultural cooperative, the political party, the church, the professional association, and so forth.

These enclaves of power, at times antagonistic, at times synergetic, tend, in general, to form coalitions, which are supported and effectuated by both formal and informal, visible and invisible, surfaced and nonsurfaced social networks, channels, or mechanisms. I define the term *Establishment* as the more or less stable coalition of the enclaves or foci of power.

Whenever things political in some country seem normal, we may assume that the coalition is doing well. In contrast, whenever we are prepared to talk about a deep political crisis, we should assume that the Establishment is undergoing a crisis, either because of *internal* trouble—namely, because some of its members have seen fit to alter their relative position within the coalition—or because of *external* trouble, because another challenger has risen who wants a share of the power. But what are the processes whereby the structure of the Establishment undergoes change? What makes for change in the relative power of some group in society?

We can easily dispose of one source of change, that which is related to intervention by some force external to the society in question, say, by some other nation-state. This is easy to understand. What we should be interested in understanding, however, is the internal process whereby the balance of power is altered. I find it useful to make a distinction, a distinction between those processes which represent a more or less smooth accommodation to growth and structural change, and those that do not.

Suppose that some country is experiencing economic growth. Assume, further, that structural change is taking place at the same rate as with economic growth. The change in living standards, the regional redistribution of economic activity, the development of new urban centers, the appearance of new functionaries, the change in the relative importance of occupational groups, and so forth cannot but give rise to new sources of political power, to new alignment of political forces, to a new internal balance of power, to a new structure of the Establishment.

The balance of power, the structure of the Establishment, may well change, however, as a result of the workings of the political process; it may arise directly from the struggle for the ascension to power. Or, what in the end amounts to the same thing, latent power may be discovered as a result of a change in the field of vision of those who possess it, or as a result of a change in their threshold of aspirations. Such changes may well be traced to external factors, such as contact with other nations.

PATERNALISTIC CAPITALISM

The Establishment in societies which do not experience a reasonable rate of economic growth exhibits such relatively high rigidity in structure as to make gradual, marginal changes in the balance of power quite unlikely. Under such conditions, any significant change in the structure of the Establishment is associated with a major political crisis, with a convulsion leading to the displacement of the insiders by the outsiders. Needless to say, every convulsive change in the *government* of a nation need not imply a change either in the structure of the State or in the structure of the Establishment. The succession of Latin American juntas need not have deeper social significance than the succession of one syndicate for another in the underworld of gangs.

In contrast, in countries which experience a reasonable rate of economic growth and structural change, the structure of power changes in a gradual, relatively unnoticed way. And so does the structure of the Establishment. But this only within limits, limits that are inherent in the social order characteristic of the society in question. A major social convulsion or political clash may indeed be expected if the emerging new sources of power are not effectively assimilated into the Establishment, on terms which do not require a basic or fundamental change in its hierarchical structure, and which, therefore, do not radically challenge the foundations of the social order.

The structure of the Establishment in any society must needs reflect the social order and the implicit distribution or structure of social power. To put it in somewhat different terms: a structure of the Establishment which violates or flies in the face of the dominant social relations in society is inconceivable. Indeed, it is an absurdity. For instance, it would be absurd to imagine that in a capitalist society the leadership of the trade unions could attain a senior position in that society's Establishment. Thus, it should be clear that the concept of the Establishment, if it is to be an effective tool of analysis, must be coordinated with that of the Ruling Class.

* * * * *

The concept of the Establishment provides a direct interpretation of the processes of influence over the vital socioeconomic processes in general, and over the State in particular. In contrast, the Marxian concept of the ruling class provides an indirect interpretation of these same processes—indirect in the sense that it may be conceived of as specifying the mechanism that places some more or less flexible limitations on the make-up or the behavior of the Establishment, in the context of any one given social order. The two levels of analysis may be reconciled along the following lines. To each type of social order there corresponds a unique class structure, unless, of course, one can effectively define the limiting case of a classless society. The class structure reflects the structure of social relations as they are shaped in the process of production—that is to say, in the ubiquitous process of confrontation of society with the natural environment in which it is embedded. According to the strict Marxian version, the "material means of production," the productive apparatus of a society along with the relevant technology, determine uniquely the social relations in the process of production and, therefore, the class structure and the social order. If we are prepared to adopt a looser version, and argue that the material means of production determine only a more or less restricted set of possibilities for the social order, then the proposition seems almost self-evident.

On this more flexible interpretation of the relationship between means of production and class structure, we may proceed to define the concept of the dominant class. In any class society, there emerges a dominant class by virtue of its control over the productive apparatus, as well as by its qualitatively distinct and quantitatively superior claims on the social product. There exist, correspondingly, subordinate as well as intermediate classes.

PATERNALISTIC CAPITALISM

The dominant class must also be the ruling class. It can hardly expect to maintain its position of dominance unless it is capable of exercising a decisive degree of political power over the State. This it can achieve only by possessing and maintaining a dominant standing in the Establishment.

This does not exclude the possibility of—indeed it is consistent with—an expanded and quite heterogeneous structure of the Establishment. What it does do is to place some distinct limitations on the hierarchy within the Establishment and on the behavior of its members.

It is appropriate to distinguish, in general, among the economic elites, the political elites, and the state elites, notwithstanding the fact that in some societies they may merge into a single, undifferentiated elite. Where they are distinct, it should be expected that the economic elite will have the dominant or most senior position in the Establishment because the economic elite springs directly from the dominant class. It should also be expected that the most prestigious component of the political elite and of the state elite will hold a prominent position in the Establishment. Needless to say, the relative importance of the state elite or the political elite in the Establishment depends both on the relative importance of the functions within the purview of the State and on the characteristics of the political order. Although it may be difficult to generalize about the relative power of the political and the state elites within the Establishment, we are in a position to define their specific role in general terms. Their role is instrumental to the maintenance of the prevalent social order. This is quite obvious in the case of the state elite, whose main tasks are internal security and justice, social and economic management (more prevalent in planned or centralized economies than in market economies), the management of national security, and the management of information, communications, and education (again, more prevalent in authoritarian societies than in democratic ones, but by no means absent in the latter). It is not equally obvious in the case of the political elite, for in democratic political systems there exist parties advocating positions distinctly hostile to the interests of the dominant class. How can one argue that these political parties are instrumental to the maintenance of a social order that they are set upon undermining?

The general answer is quite straightforward. The leaders of political parties which advocate radical changes in the social order cannot be expected to be members of the Establishment. For instance, the leaders of the Italian Communist Party are not and cannot be expected to be members of the contemporary Italian Establishment. In sharp contrast, the leaders of the Christian Democratic Party are essential components of that Establishment—indeed, they are the chosen instruments of the Italian ruling class. This general response to the question needs some qualifications. For example, it is quite possible for the leadership of a political party to belong to the Establishment, in some capacity, even if the party advocates radical change, provided it is quite clear that the party does not intend to carry through after achieving power. This, on the whole, has been the characteristic behavior of social-democratic leaders in contemporary Europe. "For their part . . . social-democratic leaders, in their moment of victory, and even more so after, have generally been most concerned to reassure the dominant classes and the business elites as to their intentions, to stress that they conceived their task in 'national' and not in 'class' terms, to insist that their assumption of office held no threat to business; and, in the same vein, they have equally been concerned to urge upon the working classes generally the virtues of patience, discipline and hard work, to warn them that electoral victory and the achievement of office by their own leaders must on no account serve as an encouragement to the militant assertion of working-class demands upon employers, propertied interests and the government itself, and to emphasize that the new ministers, faced with immense responsibilities, burdens and problems, must not be impeded in their purpose by unreasonable and unrealistic pressures."[7]

These remarks suggest how flexible the Establishment can be. Indeed, it may even include the leadership of pressure groups or organizations antagonistic or potentially antagonistic to the dominant class and to the social order. Such members of the Establishment may be considered junior or contingent members—their continued participation is contingent upon their continued good behavior. Junior or contingent membership is conferred when an accommodation is reached between the senior members and new entrants in terms which, though admitting the new entrants some degree of influence over the vital economic and social processes, does not legitimize or formalize this influence. In some sense, then, contingent members of the Establishment are assimilated into it on terms which, generally speaking, are acceptable to the senior members.

An outstanding example is provided by the leadership of labor unions in the United States. Labor, having satisfied the necessary conditions for junior or contingent membership, has achieved just that. Industrial peace has been achieved in the United States—and more generally in the advanced capitalist world—on terms which amount to the assimilation of organized labor leadership into the ruling coalition, on terms acceptable to those who have the focal control.

Finally, it should be stressed that the Establishment hierarchy is unique. Not a command structure, the Establishment relies on bargaining processes among its various components. Many accommodations can be reached, subject to one limitation: that the social order will not be placed in quandary.

In this proposal concerning the relationship between the

[7] *Ibid.*, p. 99.

dominant class and the Establishment there is a missing link. In what ways can the dominant class ensure that the political elite and the state elite—which are, on the whole, strongly represented in the Establishment—will in fact be *instrumental* in maintaining the social order? Unless this can be guaranteed, the dominant class will not also be a ruling class. And if it fails to be that, it will soon cease being a dominant class. The answer must be sought in two directions: first, in the mechanisms of selection or recruitment of the political and state elites, and second, in the indoctrination of the populace at large. The ideology of the ruling class, and the legitimacy of the norms that guide behavior within the social order, must be accepted by even the subordinate classes because unless a proper ideological climate is created, the foundations of the dominance of the ruling class will be undermined.

Penetration of the Establishment and indoctrination of the populace are necessary conditions for the continued supremacy of any dominant class.[8]

[8] In this section I have attempted a reconciliation between the concept of the ruling class and that of the power elite, C. Wright Mills' favorite term. His comments on this matter (*The Power Elite* [London, Oxford, & New York: Oxford University Press, 1959], p. 277) are worth repeating here. " 'Ruling class' is a badly loaded phrase. 'Class' is an economic term; 'rule' a political one. The phrase, 'ruling class,' thus contains the theory that an economic class rules politically. That short-cut theory may or may not at times be true, but we do not want to carry that one rather simple theory about in the terms that we use to define our problems; we wish to state the theories explicitly, using the terms of more precise and unilateral meaning. Specifically, the phrase 'ruling class,' in its common political connotations, does not allow enough autonomy to the political order and its agents, and it says nothing about the military as such . . . we do not accept as adequate the simple view that high economic men unilaterally make all decisions of national consequence. We hold that such a simple view of 'economic determinism' must be elaborated by 'political determinism' and 'military determinism'; that the higher agents of each of these three domains now often have a noticeable degree of autonomy; and that only in the often intricate ways of coalition do they make up and carry through the most important decisions. Those are the major reasons we prefer 'power elite' to 'ruling class' as a characterizing phrase for the higher circles when we consider them in terms of power." My definition of *Establishment* has the kind of flexibility in structure and behavior that is suggested by Mills' *power elite*. It relates to the "dominant class" defined in terms of the elemental structure of the economy in the following fashion: The

*THE ESTABLISHMENT IN THE CAPITALIST METROPOLIS

Does a dominant class exist in America? This question would be considered naive in any country other than America itself. It is a basic element of the American creed that American society is fundamentally a classless society—classless in the sense that there does not exist a cohesive enough economic elite which is capable of dominating the course of the nation. I share the view that this interpretation of American society is naive. "It may readily be granted that there does exist a plurality of economic elites; . . . and that despite the integrating tendencies of advanced capitalism these elites constitute distinct groupings and interests, whose competition greatly affects the political process. This 'elite pluralism' does not, however, prevent the separate elites in capitalist society from constituting a dominant class, possessed of a high degree of cohesion and solidarity, with common interests and common purposes which far transcend their specific differences and disagreements."[9]

G. William Domhoff has reached some important, though not surprising conclusions. "The consistency of our findings by different methods suggests the existence of an upper class which can be defined, operationally speaking, by its several indicators. . . . The American upper class is based upon large corporate wealth that is looked after by male members of the intermarrying families that are its basis. . . . It can be argued that the upper class is more cohesive than any other level of the American social hierarchy. Its smaller size, greater wealth, different sources of income (stocks and bonds), different

"dominant class" becomes the "ruling class" only if it can adequately penetrate the political system and the state system. This it can achieve by possessing and maintaining a dominant position in the Establishment. When it fails to achieve that, it ceases being not only the "ruling" class but, also the "dominant" class — which implies a major change in the social order.

[9] Miliband, *The State in Capitalist Society*, pp. 47–48.

schooling, different leisure activities, and different occupations, not to mention its complicated web of intermarriages, are among the evidences of this statement. I also think that there is ample evidence for asserting that an upper class exists in American consciousness. We know *they* exist. . . . And *they* know *they* are members of a privileged social class." [10]

But what about the Establishment in the United States, the more or less stable coalition of power enclaves that effectively influences its vital social, economic, political processes? It is worth our while to turn to a truly impressive short sketch of the American Establishment's history by C. Wright Mills.

"We study history, it has been said, to rid ourselves of it, and the history of the power elite is a clear case for which this maxim is correct. Like the tempo of American life in general, the long-term trends of the power structure have been greatly speeded up since World War II, and certain newer trends within and between the dominant institutions have also set the shape of the power elite and given historically specific meaning to its fifth epoch.

"I. In so far as the structural clue to the power elite today lies in the political order, that clue is the decline of politics as genuine and public debate of alternative decisions—with nationally responsible and policy-coherent parties and with autonomous organizations connecting the lower and middle levels of power with the top levels of decision. America is now in considerable part more a formal political democracy than a democratic social structure, and even the formal political mechanics are weak.

"The long-time tendency of business and government to become more intricately and deeply involved with each other has, in the fifth epoch, reached a new point of explicitness. The two cannot now be seen clearly as two distinct worlds. It is in terms

[10] *The Higher Circles: The Governing Class in America* (New York: Random House, 1970), pp. 32, 56, 97–98.

of the executive agencies of the state that the rapprochement has proceeded most decisively. The growth of the executive branch of the government, with its agencies that patrol the complex economy, does not merely mean the 'enlargement of government' as some sort of autonomous bureaucracy: it has meant the ascendancy of the corporation's man as a political eminence.

"During the New Deal the corporate chieftains joined the political directorate; as of World War II they have come to dominate it. Long interlocked with government, now they have moved into quite full direction of the economy of the war effort and of the postwar era. This shift of the corporation executives into the political directorate has accelerated the long-term relegation of the professional politicians in the Congress to the middle levels of power.

"II. In so far as the structural clue to the power elite today lies in the enlarged and military state, that clue becomes evident in the military ascendancy. The warlords have gained decisive political relevance, and the military structure of America is now in considerable part a political structure. The seemingly permanent military threat places a premium on the military and upon their control of men, materiel, money, and power; virtually all political and economic actions are now judged in terms of military definitions of reality: the higher warlords have ascended to a firm position within the power elite of the fifth epoch.

"In part at least this has resulted from one simple historical fact, pivotal for the years since 1939: the focus of elite attention has been shifted from domestic problems, centered in the 'thirties around slump, to international problems, centered in the 'forties and 'fifties around war. Since the governing apparatus of the United States has by long historic usage been adapted to and shaped by domestic clash and balance, it has not, from any angle, had suitable agencies and traditions for the handling of international problems. Such formal democratic mechanics as had arisen in the century and a half of national development prior to 1941, had not been extended to the American handling of international affairs. It is, in considerable part, in this vacuum that the power elite has grown.

"III. In so far as the structural clue to the power elite today lies in the economic order, that clue is the fact that the economy is at once a permanent-war economy and a private-corporation economy. American capitalism is now in considerable part a military capitalism, and the most important relation of the big corporation to the state rests on the coincidence of interests between military and corporate needs as defined by warlords and corporate rich. Within the elite as a whole, this coincidence of interest between the high military and the corporate chieftains strengthens both of them and further subordinates the role of the merely political men. Not politicians, but corporate executives, sit with the military and plan the organization of war effort.

"The shape and meaning of the power elite today can be understood only when these three sets of structural trends are seen at their point of coincidence: the military capitalism of private corporations exists in a weakened and formal democratic system containing a military order already quite political in outlook and demeanor. Accordingly, at the top of this structure, the power elite has been shaped by the coincidence of interest between those who control the major means of production and those who control the newly enlarged means of violence; from the decline of the professional politician and the rise to explicit political command of the corporate chieftains and the professional warlords; from the absence of any genuine civil service of skill and integrity, independent of vested interests.

"The power elite is composed of political, economic, and military men, but this instituted elite is frequently in some tension: it comes together only on certain coinciding points and only on certain occasions of 'crisis.' In the long peace of the nineteenth century, the military were not in the high councils of state, not of the political directorate, and neither were the economic men—they made raids upon the state but they did not join its directorate. During the 'thirties, the political man was ascendant. Now the military and the corporate men are in top positions.

"Of the three types of circle that compose the power elite today, it is the military that has benefited the most in its enhanced power, although the corporate circles have also become more explicitly intrenched in the more public decision-making circles. It is the professional politician that has lost the most, so much that in examining the events and decisions, one is tempted to speak of a political vacuum in which the corporate rich and the high warlord, in their coinciding interests, rule.

"It should not be said that the three 'take turns' in carrying the initiative, for the mechanics of the power elite are not often as deliberate as that would imply. At times, of course, it is—as when political men, thinking they can borrow the prestige of generals, find that they must pay for it, or as when during big slumps, economic men feel the need of a politician at once safe and possessing vote appeal. Today all three are involved in virtually all widely ramifying decisions. Which of the three types seems to lead depends upon 'the tasks of the period' as they, the elite, define them. Just now, these tasks center upon 'defense' and international affairs. Accordingly, as we have seen, the military are ascendant in two senses: as personnel and as justifying ideology. That is why, just now, we can most easily specify the unity and the shape of the power elite in terms of the military ascendancy." [11]

C. Wright Mills' analysis, as it concerns the "fifth epoch"—dating back to 1956—has been amply confirmed by the events of the last fifteen years.

[11] Mills, The Power Elite, pp. 274–277.

* * * * *

The apex of the pyramid of power within the contemporary American Establishment is occupied by the corporate managerial-capitalist elite. Occupying the seat of the most senior partner, it clearly does not sit alone. Side by side with the manager of the giant modern corporate enterprise is a segment of the state elite which is responsible for the management of national security. The national security managers are the product of the Second World War and of the era of the Cold War. In thirty years of global conflict they have risen to a position of pre-eminence in the Establishment in a society that day by day is taking on all the characteristics of a militaristic order.

In the words of Richard Barnet, "the principal militarists in America wear three-button suits. They are civilians in everything but outlook. Not the generals but the National Security Managers—the politicians, businessmen, and civil servants rotate through the paneled offices of the Pentagon, the State Department, the Central Intelligence Agency, the Atomic Energy Commission, and the White House—have been in charge of national-security policy. . . . Civilian control of the military has been maintained throughout the long years of the Cold War, but the price has been the militarization of the civilian leadership. Generals and Admirals continue to take orders from the President as Commander-in-Chief, but the President spends about 90 percent of his time building and . . . projecting America's military power. Increasingly the civilians have come to see the world through military eyes. . . . Indeed, there is considerable evidence that the civilian managers, particularly at the beginning of the postwar period, have been far readier than the military to commit American forces to actual combat. Apprenticed to the military in World

War II, the top civilian national-security elite absorbed the basic military outlook but not the soldier's professional caution. . . . The militarized civilians have surpassed the military themselves in embracing a 'realism' which envisages no alternative to an escalating arms race but annihilation, perpetuates an aimless war by calling it a commitment, and measures a nation's greatness in megatons." [12]

But who are the National Security Managers? "Since 1940 about 400 individuals have held the top civilian national-security positions. These men have defined the threats for the nation, made the commitments that were supposed to meet these threats, and determined the size of the armed forces. They have been above electoral politics." They "have come from executive suites and law offices within shouting distance of one another in fifteen city blocks in New York, Washington, Detroit, Chicago, and Boston. It is not surprising that they emerge from homogeneous backgrounds and virtually identical careers with a standard way of looking at the world. They may argue with one another about means but not about ends. . . . It is hardly surprising that those who have prospered equate the national interest with the status quo. When the term is stripped of geopolitical metaphor and ideological gloss, national security means nothing more complicated than making sure that the American Way of Life continues undisturbed by foreign challengers."

More specifically, "if we take a look at the men who have held the very top positions, the Secretaries and Under Secretaries of State and Defense, the Secretaries of the three services, the Chairman of the Atomic Energy Commission, and the Director of the CIA, we find that out of ninety-one individuals who held these offices during the period 1940–1967, seventy of them were from the ranks of big business or high finance, including eight out of ten Secretaries of Defense,

[12] The Economy of Death, pp. 79, 82, 83, 84.

116

The State

seven out of eight Secretaries of the Air Force, every Secretary of the Navy, eight out of nine Secretaries of the Army, every Deputy Secretary of Defense, three out of five Directors of the CIA, and three out of five Chairmen of the Atomic Energy Commission." [13]

Thus, it seems that the national security managers form a social elite that to all intents and purposes is indistinguishable from the top echelon of the corporate managerial-capitalist elite. And though we may wish to maintain the distinction between the two, it is essential that we do not put too much stress on it. We are dealing, in fact, with the same social group in two distinct roles.

But what about the military bureaucracy? Its top echelons, represented by the Joint Chiefs of Staff and other senior officers, must undoubtedly be included in the national security managerial group. And in this capacity, the top echelon of the military bureaucracy can claim a prominent position in the establishment of contemporary America. "The Joint Chiefs of Staff possess sufficient power today so that the President of the United States cannot simply order them. . . . There is a deep fear pervading the civilian leadership that the military, if sufficiently provoked, might pit their professional credentials against the 'politicians' in a public confrontation." [14] In the words of General David M. Shoup, "the military will disclaim any excess of power or influence on their part. They will point to their small numbers, low pay, and subordination to civilian masters as proof of their modest status and innocence. Nevertheless, the professional military, as a group, is probably one of the best organized and most influential of the various segments of the American scene. . . . Not many industries, institutions, or civilian branches of government have the resources, techniques, or experience in training leaders such as are now

[13] *Ibid.*, pp. 87, 88, 97–98.
[14] *Ibid.*, p. 82.

117

PATERNALISTIC CAPITALISM

employed by the armed forces in their excellent and elaborate school systems. Military leaders are taught to command large organizations and to plan big operations. They learn the techniques of influencing others. Their education is not, however, liberal or cultural. It stresses the tactics, doctrines, traditions, and codes of the military trade. It produces technicians and disciples, not philosophers. . . . More so than many large bureaucratic organizations, the defense establishment now devotes a large share of its efforts to self-perpetuation, to justifying its organizations, to preaching its doctrines, and to self-maintenance and management. Warfare becomes an extension of war games and field tests. War justifies the existence of the establishment, provides experience for the military novice, and challenges for the senior officer. . . . Standing closely behind these leaders, encouraging and prompting them, are the rich and powerful defense industries." [15]

I argued above that the social overlap between the corporate managerial-capitalist elite and the civilian component of the national security managerial group was so great as to render the distinction between them somewhat irrelevant. Actually, much the same can be said about the relations between the top echelons of the military hierarchy and the corporate elite. For the distinctive characteristic of the American establishment during its "fifth epoch" is the interchangeability of the top roles. This leads C. Wright Mills to talk about an inner core of the power elite, or the Establishment. "The inner core of the power elite consists, first, of those who interchange commanding roles at the top of one dominant institutional order with those in another: the admiral who is also a banker and a lawyer and who heads up an important federal commission; the corporation executive whose company was one of the two or three leading war material producers who is now the

[15] "The New American Militarism," *The Atlantic*, Vol. 223, No. 4, April 1969, pp. 53, 56.

Secretary of Defense; the wartime general who dons civilian clothes to sit on the political directorate and then becomes a member of the board of directors of a leading economic corporation. Although the executive who becomes a general, the general who becomes a statesman, the statesman who becomes a banker, see much more than the ordinary man in their ordinary environments, still the perspectives of even such men often remain tied to their dominant locales. In their very career, however, they interchange roles within the big three and thus readily transcend the particularity of interest in any one of these institutional milieux. By their very careers and activities, they lace the three types of milieux together. They are, accordingly, the core members of the power elite." [16]

Thus, the focus of power in the contemporary American Establishment rests with the corporate managerial-capitalist elite, the civilian nonbureaucratic component of the national security managerial group, the top echelons of the bureaucracy charged with the management of national security, and especially, of course, the military bureaucracy. Of these components of the Establishment, the most senior, in a truly pervasive sense, is the corporate elite. The corporate elite underlies and is, in the last analysis, identified with all of them. The American dominant class now rules by having occupied the "core" of the Establishment in an effectively comprehensive, all-enveloping way.

Prominent, but at the middle range of importance in the Establishment, are the other components of the state elite—that is to say, the state elite other than those identified with the management of national security. The political elite also seems to have been relegated to this middle range of power. Especially significant is the visible, dramatic decline in the power of Congress to affect the executive's decisions on major issues of foreign policy and national security.

[16] *The Power Elite*, pp. 288–289.

But there exist genuine junior or contingent members of the American Establishment. The most clearly visible are organized labor and a large component of the scientific estate. From hard hats to think tank experts—one finds a large and influential component of American Society participating in, benefiting from, and contributing to the American Way of Life as it has been defined by the senior partners of the U.S. Establishment. "Scientists from America and the capitalist countries have placed themselves in the service of pentagonism, but on the other end of the social scale the workers of the United States are doing the same thing. Mr. Meany, the president of the AFL-CIO, enthusiastically approved his country's intervention in the Dominican Republic, on the grounds that the revolution of April 1965 in that little Antillean country was communist. In reality, it was a matter of the AFL-CIO—as an organized mass within a pentagonized society—responding to the division of activities imposed by pentagonism: freedom of action for Americans within the United States in exchange for support of pentagonism outside the country." [17]

It has become obvious even to the common citizen—especially after the publication of the Pentagon Papers—that the power of the U.S. Establishment is overwhelming. It has made a mockery of the traditional, constitutional structure of political power, having led the country into a protracted and costly war which has not had the direct, official consent of Congress.

The American Establishment today is at once capitalistic and militaristic. If the present trends are not reversed, it will soon also be unmistakably totalitarian.

[17] Juan Bosch, *Pentagonism* (New York: Grove Press, 1968), pp. 59–60.

Peaceful Coexistence and Counter-Revolution

An increasingly militarized society is of necessity involved in war, actual or potential. The two global powers, the United States and the Soviet Union, have in fact been engaged in war ever since the death of President Roosevelt. It has been called the Cold War, but "cold" it actually almost never was. Armed confrontations directly or indirectly involving the two super-powers have studded the last quarter century and have taken a spectacular toll of life and property. The only sense in which the war could be called cold is that the recourse to arms has been intentionally localized.

There are two clearly distinguishable periods in the relations between the two giants: the period from Roosevelt's death to August 5, 1963 (the date of the signing of the Moscow treaty on nuclear tests), and the period that follows the signing of this treaty. The first period, which André Fontaine believes may be characterized as the Third World War, was a period of confrontation. The second period is called, euphemistically, the period of peaceful coexistence. Peaceful coexistence includes by now eight years of bitter and costly war in Indochina, though the coexistence is, of course, more or less peaceful in Europe. Furthermore, and despite Soviet support of North Vietnam, the confrontation in Indochina is not primarily a confrontation between the two super-powers. It is primarily a continuation, in a particularly acute form, of the policy of the United States to contain revolution. This policy of counter-revolution provides the unifying theme of the postwar behavior of the United States—through both the period of confrontation and the period of peaceful coexistence with the Soviet Union.

* * * * *

Peaceful coexistence for the United States and the Soviet Union has meant no more than that the deadly chess game has been played by relatively well-observed rules. They include mutual respect of the other's supremacy within a well-defined sphere of influence; prevention, to the extent possible, of the rise of another super-power; elimination of neutralism; and, finally, mutual restraint in regions where they challenge each other for definition of a new equilbrium. The rule kit may, before long, include some explicit rules limiting the competition between them in developing their respective arsenals. Of course, the stability of this evolving system of rules is threatened both by centrifugal tendencies within the Cold War blocs, and by "extremist" tendencies within the establishments of the super-powers, when tensions between them become high.

In the context of peaceful coexistence, there is a clearly discernible reflective tendency in the behavior of each super-power within its sphere of influence. When events take place in one bloc which loosen up the control of the super-power over its allies (satellites), similar relaxation phenomena tend to take place on the other side of the fence. In contrast, when one of the super-powers takes repressive measures, they are countered by the other super-power almost immediately.

And it is possible, in principle, to interpret even the era of confrontation in these terms of action and response. But caution is required in extending to the period of confrontation an interpretive scheme that seems to fit so well the behavior pattern of the two super-powers in the era of peaceful coexistence. It would be an error to imagine that in the period of confrontation—the period that shaped the behavior patterns of the two super-powers—action and response were "randomly" distributed. Although historians will continue the debate for years to come, it seems rather clear on the basis of available evidence that in the era of confrontation the *action* was American and the *response* Russian.

Furthermore, as peaceful coexistence extends into the seventies, the presence of a third super-power, China, will increasingly influence the behavior of the United States and the Soviet Union because it increasingly becomes important for each of the three super-powers to prevent a coalition between the other two.

The prevailing view in the United States, especially during the era of confrontation, has been that the Soviet Union is an expansionist imperial power. Consider Adlai Stevenson's statement in the United Nations on October 23, 1962, in connection with the naval blockade against Cuba: "The record is clear: treaties, agreements, pledges and the morals of international relations were never an obstacle to the Soviet Union under Stalin. . . . No one can question that Chairman Khrushchev has altered many things in the Soviet Union. But there is one thing he has not altered—and that is the basic drive to abolish the world of the Charter, to destroy the hope of a pluralistic world order. . . . It is this which has shadowed the world since the end of the Second World War—which has dimmed our hopes of peace and progress, which has forced those nations determined to defend their freedom to take measures in their own self-defense. . . . Our response to the *remorseless Soviet expansionism* has taken many forms. We have sought loyally to support the United Nations, to be faithful to the world of the Charter, and to build an operating system that acts, and does not talk for peace." [1] This piece of rhetoric sums up succinctly the official American interpretation placed on the global role of the Soviet Union. That the United States had instituted the blockade in disregard of the United Nations, and that it had organized the ill-fated invasion of the Bay of Pigs eighteen months earlier—these facts were glossed over.

But the belief in Russia's readiness to break "treaties, agreements, pledges and the morals of international relations" goes all the way back to the beginnings of the confrontation. And it reflects the contradiction between what was secretly agreed upon between Churchill and Stalin in Moscow in October 1944, and the Yalta Declaration. Churchill describes his meeting with Stalin in Moscow on October 9, 1944, as follows: "The moment was apt for business, so I said, 'let us settle about our affairs in the Balkans. Your armies are in Rumania and Bulgaria. We have interests, missions and agents there. Don't let us get at cross-purposes in small ways. So far as Britain and Russia are concerned, how would it do for you to have ninety per cent predominance in Rumania, for us to have ninety per cent of the say in Greece, and go fifty-fifty

[1] As quoted in David Horowitz, *From Yalta to Vietnam* (Penguin Books, 1969), p. 12. The emphasis is mine.

124

about Yugoslavia?' While this was being transacted I wrote out on a half-sheet of paper:

Rumania	
Russia	90%
The others	10%
Greece	
Great Britain (in accord with U.S.A.)	90%
Russia	10%
Yugoslavia	50%–50%
Hungary	50%–50%
Bulgaria	
Russia	75%
The others	25%

"I pushed this across to Stalin who had by then heard the translation. There was a slight pause. Then he took his blue pencil and made a large tick upon it, and passed it back to us. It was settled in no more time than it takes to set it down. . . .

"After this there was a long silence. The penciled paper lay in the centre of the table. At length I said, 'Might it not be thought rather cynical if it seemed we had disposed of these issues, so fateful to millions of people, in such an offhand manner? Let us burn the paper.' 'No, you keep it,' said Stalin." [2]

Stalin lived up to this agreement in the case of Greece—a test that was to come less than two months from its conclusion. He did not lift a finger to aid the National Liberation Front–National Popular Liberation Army (EAM-ELAS) forces in their confrontation with British troops in December 1944, a confrontation that marked the beginning of the second phase of the Greek civil war. And Churchill, in gratitude, cabled Roosevelt that "Stalin adhered very strictly to the understanding." [3]

Then came Yalta. There, on February 4–11, 1945, the three powers agreed to aid the peoples of Europe "to form interim

---

[2] *The Second World War: Triumph and Tragedy* (Boston: Houghton Mifflin, 1953), pp. 227–228. For an excellent treatment of the subject, see L. S. Stavrianos, *The Balkans Since 1453* (New York: Holt, 1958).

[3] James F. Byrnes, *Speaking Frankly* (New York: Harper, 1947), p. 53.

governmental authorities broadly representative of all democratic elements in the population and pledged to the earliest possible establishment through free elections of governments responsive to the will of the people." [4] The Declaration, literally interpreted, contradicts the Churchill-Stalin Moscow agreement—an agreement on whose basis Stalin permitted the British troops to defeat the all-powerful EAM-ELAS, and urged Tito to restore the monarchy in Yugoslavia.

But the Russians did not interpret the Declaration literally. They "clung to the percentage agreement and regarded the Declaration as mere window dressing. They had scrupulously kept their hands off Greece while Churchill had battered the ELAS. Now they expected the Western powers in turn to respect their '90 per cent say' in Rumania and '75 per cent say' in Bulgaria. Consequently they were surprised and outraged when the British gradually and somewhat embarrassedly joined the United States in forgetting the percentages and insisting on fulfillment of the Declaration. The Russians refused to budge on this point because they regarded 'friendly' governments in Eastern Europe as absolutely necessary for their security. A few months later at the Potsdam Conference Stalin declared flatly: 'A freely elected government in any of these countries [in Eastern Europe] would be anti-Soviet, and that we cannot allow.' This contradiction between 'friendly' and 'freely elected' governments was the rock on which the Big Three Grand Alliance foundered as soon as this rock was laid bare by the ebb of the tide of German conquest." [5]

On August 18, 1945, Byrnes openly attacked the Russians for preparing to rig the Bulgarian elections—exactly nine days after the pulverization of Nagasaki by the second atom bomb. "Thus, on the very day when the second atomic bomb was dropped on Nagasaki, and while Washington was openly staking out its own sphere of influence in the Pacific, Presi-

[4] Stavrianos, The Balkans Since 1453, p. 829.
[5] Ibid., pp. 829–830.

dent Truman declared that the East European countries were 'not to be spheres of influence of any one power.' This was the effective end of the coalition." [6]

Actually, from the very start of his presidency, Truman initiated a new approach to the Soviet Union. It was based on two assumptions: First, that the United States had been unnecessarily soft in its dealings with the Russians. Second, that the only language the Russians could understand was tough language—"Missouri mule-driver's language," as Drew Pearson characterized it. This change in tone could hardly be missed by the Soviet Union. In fact, the new posture of the United States led to the clash between Henry Wallace and President Truman. On July 23, 1946, Wallace, then Secretary of Commerce, wrote to him: "How do American actions since V-J Day appear to other nations? I mean by actions the concrete things like $13 billion for the War and Navy Departments, the Bikini tests of the atomic bomb and continued production of bombs, the plan to arm Latin America with our weapons, production of B-29s and planned production of B-36s and the effort to secure air bases spread over half the globe from which the other half of the globe can be bombed. I cannot but feel that these actions must make it look to the rest of the world as if we were only paying lip service to peace at the conference table.

"These facts rather make it appear either (1) that we are preparing ourselves to win the war we regard as inevitable or (2) that we are trying to build up a predominance of force to intimidate the rest of mankind. How would it look to us if Russia had the atomic bomb and we did not, if Russia had 10,000-mile bombers and air bases within 1,000 miles of our coastlines, and we did not? . . ." [7]

Six months later, on February 24, 1947, Great Britain in-

---

[6] Horowitz, *From Yalta to Vietnam*, p. 57.

[7] As quoted in *ibid.*, p. 60.

formed the United States that she was unable to continue the policing of Greece and Turkey. On March 12, 1947, President Truman enunciated his Doctrine. On the strength of this Doctrine, the United States poured extensive economic and military aid into Greece, and made it possible for the Greek monarchy to win a decisive victory over the EAM-ELAS forces. In his address to a joint session of Congress, President Truman said:

"At the present moment in world history nearly every nation must choose between alternative ways of life. The choice is too often not a free one.

"One way of life is based upon the will of the majority, and is distinguished by free institutions, representative government, free elections, guarantees of individual liberty, freedom of speech and religion, and freedom from oppression.

"The second way of life is based upon the will of the minority forcibly imposed upon the majority. It relies upon terror and oppression of controlled press and radio; fixed elections, and the suppression of personal freedoms.

"I believe it must be the policy of the United States to support free peoples who are resisting attempted subjugation by armed minorities or by outside pressure." [8]

Notwithstanding the rhetoric about democracy, the U.S. intervention in Greece represented above all a counter-revolutionary action in the service of the strategic and economic interests of the United States in the eastern Mediterranean and the Middle East. This takes on special importance, since in the case of Greece there was no danger of Russian intervention or involvement: "the Soviets in fact were giving neither aid nor direction. A few months later they would vainly seek to persuade Yugoslavia to cut off the substantial aid which they were giving. 'What do you think,' Stalin ex-

[8] Harry S. Truman, Address before Joint Session of Congress, March 12, 1947.

claimed to the Yugoslav vice-premier in early 1948, 'that Great Britain and the United States—the United States, the most powerful state in the world—will permit you to break their line of communication in the Mediterranean? And we have no navy. The uprising in Greece must be stopped, and as quickly as possible.' Indeed, the Soviet attitude toward Greece conformed perfectly to the Stalinist pattern. Since the Greek guerrillas had taken action independent of the Red army and Stalin's direction, the Kremlin viewed them as a nuisance and a possible threat to the diplomatic relations of the Soviet Union. Stalin saw them as potential clients of the Yugoslavs, whose claims to a role of independent political leadership in the Balkans he was already attempting to crush." [9]

The intervention in Greece, under the Truman Doctrine, represents the critical turning point in the postwar foreign policy of the United States. For it "provided Truman with the occasion to declare that the world was divided between alternative 'ways of life' and to proclaim an ideological crusade against the 'un-American way.' " [10] In this sense it was a call for a confrontation with the communist world—and, of course, with the Soviet Union itself. Furthermore, it provided a "model for U.S. relations toward civil wars and insurgencies. . . . The American experience in Greece not only set the pattern for subsequent interventions in internal wars but also suggested the criteria for assessing the success or failure of counterinsurgency operations. Greece was the first major police task which the United States took on in the postwar world. One of the most important consequences of the American involvement in Greece in the 1940's was the development of new bureaucracies specializing in military assistance, police administration, and economic aid, committed to an analysis of

[9] Richard J. Barnet, *Intervention and Revolution* (Cleveland & New York: World, 1968), p. 121.
[10] Horowitz, *From Yalta to Vietnam*, p. 63.

revolution and a set of responses for dealing with it that would be applied to many different conflicts in the next twenty years." [11]

The Soviet response, as should have been expected, was severe. The coalition regimes in Eastern Europe were converted into militant communist regimes with close ties to Moscow—Hungary, Bulgaria, and Poland in 1947 and Czechoslovakia in 1948. In fact, "Eastern Europe in the early summer of 1947 had by no means reached full satellite status. A democratic government existed in Prague; in Warsaw all manner of Polish nationalists, inside and outside the Communist Party, had not yet been brought to heel; in Yugoslavia, unknown to the West, Tito . . . was stirring the Bulgarian and Hungarian Communists with ideas about a Balkan communist alliance, quasi-independent of Moscow." [12] The Russian response was deeply nationalistic and conservative. Russia's bitter attack on Tito and Titoism, the harshness with which she dealt with her own satellites, had little to do with communist ideology as such. Rather, orthodox communist ideology became an instrument for buttressing the fortress Russia by eliminating or attempting to eliminate all nationalist elements in her sphere of influence. The conscious pursuit of this policy was a natural outgrowth of the crusading policeman's role assumed by the United States in the Truman years.

During those years the foundations for the "reflective" tendency of the two blocs were laid. To the Marshall Plan the Soviet Union responded by forming the Cominform. The Marshall Plan—ostensibly designed to aid Western Europe in its "enterprise of reconstruction"—bypassed the mechanisms of the United Nations. It was announced on June 5, 1947. Earlier in May, Dean Acheson, arguing in favor of the Plan, had claimed that "these measures of relief and reconstruction

---

[11] Barnet, *Intervention and Revolution*, p. 97.
[12] W. W. Rostow, *The United States in the World Arena* (New York: Harper, 1960), p. 212.

have been only in part suggested by humanitarians. Your Congress has authorized and your Government is carrying out, a policy of relief and reconstruction today chiefly as a matter of national self-interest. . . . *Free peoples who are seeking to preserve their independence and democratic institutions and human freedoms against totalitarian pressures, either internal or external, will receive top priority for American aid."* [13] And in response, the Cominform—established on October 5, 1947 —issued a statement a month later in which it claimed that "two opposite political lines have formed. On the one side the policy of the USSR and democratic countries directed toward undermining imperialism and strengthening democracy, on the other side is the policy of the USA and England directed toward strengthening imperialism and strangling democracy. . . . The Truman-Marshall plan is only a constituent part, the European section of the general plan of world expansionist policy carried on by the United States in all parts of the world." [14]

The North Atlantic Treaty Organization was signed on April 4, 1949. "Moscow's reaction to the signing of the Washington pact was naturally violent. In a note dated April 1, the Soviet Foreign Minister contended that it was 'obviously aggressive' and that it violated the Potsdam Agreements as well as the Anglo and French-Russian treaties." [15] Yet the Warsaw Pact was not born until much later, when in May 1955 West Germany was brought into the Western military alliance. The inclusion of West Germany in NATO carried the division of Europe into two military blocs to a climax. "Thus the Truman Doctrine of a world divided into two opposing camps proved to be a self-fulfilling prophecy: given the mentality of the

[13] Kenneth Ingram, *History of the Cold War* (London: Darweu Finlayson, 1955), pp. 58–59.
[14] F. L. Schuman, *Russia Since 1917* (New York: Knopf, 1957), pp. 362–363.
[15] André Fontaine, *History of the Cold War*, Volume I, (New York: Vintage Books, 1970), p. 368.

Russian leaders, the whole postwar United States policy of facing the Soviets with an 'iron fist' and 'strong language,' while at the same time making it as difficult as possible for them to carry out the work of reconstruction, ensured the 'expansion' that the policy, allegedly, had been designed to prevent." [16]

On a global scale, the confrontation between the two super-powers reached its climax in 1962, over Cuba. And then, in the summer of 1963, with the signing of the Moscow treaty on nuclear tests, a new climate was ushered in, the climate of Peaceful Coexistence.

There is much evidence in support of the view that, during the era of confrontation, the Soviet Union did not act as an expansionist power.[17] The widely and tenaciously held judgment to the contrary is based undoubtedly on an uncritical and unwarranted identification of the Soviet Union, as a national power, with world communism and with global revolution.

Eight years of peaceful coexistence have brought the two super-powers much closer together, especially in Europe. Detente in the context of a consolidation of the division of Europe and of more effective control over allies and satellites is now characteristic of the behavior of both the United States and the Soviet Union since 1963.

[16] Horowitz, *From Yalta to Vietnam*, p. 90.
[17] Whether this was due to lack of power or lack of will is a matter that cannot be settled in a manner satisfactory for all students of Russian foreign policy.

Peaceful Coexistence and Counter-Revolution

The recent cases of Greece and Czechoslovakia deserve special mention in this connection: The post–civil war police state of Greece was loosened up through the election of the Center Union Party and most of the repressive measures and laws executed during and after the civil war were relaxed. Greece was on its way to becoming a more democratic, progressive, and sovereign country. But the U.S. national security managers considered these developments as dangerous for NATO, fearing an opening to the Left and war in Cyprus. On July 15, 1965, the King, in close association with the United States Services in Greece, dismissed the Center Union government, despite its overwhelming popular support. A succession of puppet governments appointed by the King failed to get popular acceptance of the change. The date of elections was set, with all indications pointing to a triumph of the Center Union. The generals, the big junta, were debating the date for execution of plan PROMETHEUS, the code name for a NATO-elaborated military plan to seize power in Greece, when in the interim, the colonels supported both by the Pentagon and the CIA beat the generals and the King to the punch on April 21, 1967, through the forceful seizure of power and the establishment of a military dictatorship.

A somewhat similar process of democratization and assertion of national self-determination in the context of the Warsaw Pact was under way in Czechoslovakia. The Soviet Union, fearful that the structure of control within the Warsaw Pact bloc would be endangered, occupied Czechoslovakia. Despite their superficial differences, the events in Czechoslovakia are in broad perspective a replica of and response to the events in Greece.

The cases of Greece and Czechoslovakia are of particular significance to the Europeans. Super-power intervention in both cases has all the characteristics of bloc-internal police action. Both were intentionally misrepresented. Officially, the

United States let it be understood in European government circles that the assumption of power by the Greek military junta was intended to prevent anarchy and a dangerous opening to the communist Left, which would have corroded the strategic position of NATO in the Eastern Mediterranean basin. And Moscow lost no opportunity in telling its people and the people of its satellites that the invasion of Czechoslovakia became necessary in order to thwart American imperialism. Thus both super-powers interpreted their actions as bloc-defensive, indirectly accusing one another of expansionist tactics. They did not fall for their own propaganda, but rather, in a variety of ways they sanctioned each other's intervention. And this because the control of the two super-powers over their "allies" in Europe was strengthened hand in hand with the reassertion of the division of Europe into Cold War blocs—a division that reaffirms their controlling role in their respective spheres of influence.

Clearly, the Warsaw Pact invasion of Czechoslovakia breathed new life into NATO. Although, understandably, the official U.S. response to the invasion was very mild, the various political elites in Europe which are closely tied to the NATO directorate proceeded to interpret it as a threat to Western Europe—and issued an impassioned plea to the European allies to close ranks so that they could meet it effectively. Chancellor Brandt's new West German policies toward the East are no more than a confirmation of the division of Europe into two blocs, and an implicit admission that whatever rapprochement is to take place between nations belonging to the Western bloc and nations belonging to the Eastern bloc must do so under the auspices of the two super-powers whose "sovereignty" over European soil cannot and should not be challenged.

Senator Mansfield's initiative, in the spring of 1971, for the partial withdrawal of American troops from Europe was explicitly sabotaged by Moscow—which chose the very moment of congressional debate on the issue to suggest publicly the possibility of mutual reduction of military forces in Europe. Obviously, neither Moscow nor Washington desires a significant reduction in its military presence on European soil. This military presence is viewed by both of them as a necessary condition for the maintenance and extension of their control over their respective spheres of influence in Europe.

The NATO directorate, a vast military and economic complex under the direct control of the Pentagon, exercises decisive influence over the establishments of the participating Western European countries—and is indeed itself a not insignificant component of these establishments. Its network of power extends from the military elites and the top echelons of the national security bureaucracies in general, to the economic and political elites of the member nations. And the Warsaw Pact directorate, controlled by Moscow, has become by now a far more reliable instrument of control over the Soviet Union's European satellites than the local communist parties.

In contrast to the European front, where a modus vivendi has been worked out by the two super-powers, the Mediterranean basin—and especially its eastern half, with its proximity to oil and the Arab-Israeli conflict—presents the two super-powers with some serious challenges. The situation there is quite fluid, for alignments are in the making and nationalistic sentiments run high. Thus, both Moscow and Washington are engaged in a rather active game, of expansion of their military—especially naval, air, and nuclear—presence and of infiltration as a prelude to the subjugation of the Mediterranean nations, often through the engineering of coups by subservient military cliques.

The Arab-Israeli conflict is manipulated so as to produce the right political climate and the justification for the enhancement of the military posture of the two super-powers in the Mediterranean basin, without leading them into a direct "hot" confrontation. The last twenty-five years have taught the two giants how to control their competition and how to transform it into an effective instrument for the extension of their control over the geosphere.

$$* \ * \ * \ * \ *$$

The dominant dynamic on a global scale—a dynamic that transcends the relations between the two super-powers—is one of counter-revolution. Its theaters are to be found in the Mediterranean, in Latin America, in Southeast Asia, and in Africa—in the vast expanse of the Third World. The main actor, the main vehicle of this counter-revolutionary dynamic is America.

Not that the Soviet Union identifies itself with the forces of insurgency. It deals with governments and forms its alliances with them, independently of their ideological positions or internal social structure. Propaganda apart, its attitude toward Third World insurgency and revolution is as hostile as that exhibited by the United States ever since the enunciation of the Truman Doctrine. But the Soviet Union neither identifies itself with counter-insurgency, nor does it take the initiative to suppress revolution—unless it takes place in a nation or region under its own control. "Stalin's prime interest, as the Hitler-Stalin pact made unmistakably clear, was to build and defend the power of the Soviet state at any cost. To this end local communists would be sacrified unhesitatingly. But in fact the abandonment or leashing of foreign communists was hardly a sacrifice for Stalin or his successors, for a truly independent communist revolution was a threat to Soviet interests. It is no accident, as the Soviets themselves like to say, that two of the three communist governments established by local revolutionaries independent of the Red army—China and Albania—became enemies of the Soviet state, and a third, Yugoslavia, once also an enemy, is now, at best a wary neighbour. There is little doubt that Stalin would have liked to manufacture revolutions if the revolutionary governments would have been reliably subservient. . . . The postwar experience revealed that without the overwhelming power of the Red army on the scene, local revolutionaries, no matter how many years they had spent in Moscow, would not play the puppet role. Having risked their lives in the wartime resistance movements and with their own energy and skill thrown off the old regimes along with the Nazis, they were not prepared to exchange German masters for Russian. . . . Stalin . . . discouraged the French resistance and told them to line up behind General de Gaulle. He directed the Italian communists, who were in a very strong position, to come to terms with the government of Marshal Badoglio. He gave the same advice to Mao Tse-tung, urging him to submit to the Kuomintang, despite the fact that Mao's armies controlled vast portions of China and that Chiang twenty years earlier had slaughtered the Communist-party leadership. . . . Soviet policy toward the Third World has been so clearly in the tradition of self-serving Great Power politics that the Kremlin has difficulty in posing as champion of revolution." [18]

The nationalist and socialist revolutionaries of the Third World have emerged as the greatest problem of the national security managers of both super-powers. They threaten law and order, and undermine the foundations of Pax Americana. It is understandable. The revolutionaries of the Third World express forces which are by definition contradictory with the social, economic, political, and military imperium of the two super-powers. They personify the centrifugal, nationalistic quest of the peoples of the Third World in their drive for self-determination.

[18] Barnet, *Intervention and Revolution*, pp. 63–64, 65.

PATERNALISTIC CAPITALISM

Of course, the United States holds the stage as the main, global counter-revolutionary, interventionist force. Vietnam, Cambodia, Laos, Korea, the Dominican Republic, Guatemala, and Greece are some of the largest monuments erected in the wake of this counter-revolutionary expansionism of postwar America. Is this counter-revolutionary expansionism of the United States the result of cumulative "errors" of judgment; does it spring from a drive to promote the "open society"; or is it a response to a "communist conspiracy" directed by the Kremlin? To ask these questions is to answer them. Only the most naive could accept any of these interpretations of American foreign policy in the postwar era. But if there is logic and unity to the counter-revolutionary behavior of the United States, whence does it spring?

For Arthur Schlesinger, Jr., the explanation lies in the neo-imperialist expansionism of the military caste! "Yet, if the national security bureaucracy is often divided in its views, the warrior caste, as a powerful element in the bureaucracy, has had increasingly behind it the power of sheer momentum—especially in a time when new military technologies, by making America vulnerable to attack from almost any spot on the planet, gave the argument of 'national security' an unlimited application, and when duty required the military of one nation to advocate constant growth to forestall adversaries from gaining technological superiority. 'Created by wars that required it,' Schumpeter wrote of the military establishment in ancient Egypt, 'the machine now created the wars it required.' In whatever sense America can be said to be an imperial state, the active carriers of that imperialism are not our bankers or our foreign investors or our traders—not any of the conventional Marxist villains. The carriers are our politicians, our diplomats, and most particularly, our military leaders who—for military, not for economic reasons—have conned both the executive and legislative branches of government into voting enormous military appropriations and into building enormous military installations, largely irrelevant in the missile age, all over the world (and who, as the price we must pay, insist we must do nothing to offend such splendid countries as Portugal or South Africa). It is they who argue for military intervention." [19]

No one should slight the role of the military. For the modern military man—especially when he is charged with the security of an empire—is quite different from his predecessors. He deals in awesome technologies. He commands spectacular resources. Given modern war technology, the geosphere becomes necessarily his oyster. As a planner he must consider the long run. He must anticipate new weapons systems. He must anticipate political, social, economic developments, not only at home, but on a worldwide basis. And since war-preparedness—which, in the military's mind, is the basis of national security—requires total mobilization of human and material resources, he must secure his capability to effectuate a national mobilization, when it becomes necessary. This much is true. But it will not do for an explanation of the foreign policy of the United States. More is needed. First, because the United States always[20] identifies itself with socially reactionary regimes. Second, because economic infiltration, domination, and expansionism do indeed go hand in hand with military-strategic expansionism. Third, because the men who are ultimately responsible for the foreign policy and the defense strategy of the United States are not the military but the three-button suit national security managers.

For a view that is diametrically opposed to Schlesinger's we can turn to Gabriel Kolko. "I have tried to show how pervasive are the assumptions and power of those civilians who run Washington, and how they have freely utilized the Military

[19] "Vietnam and the End of the Age of Superpowers," *Harper's Magazine*, Vol. 238, March 1969, pp. 41–49.

[20] With the notable exception of Western Europe, which is not the point at issue here.

Establishment as a tool for advancing their own interests rather than the mythical independent goals of the officers. For businessmen and their political cohorts have defined the limits within which the military formulates strategy, extending their values and definitions of priorities over essentially docile generals. A closer look at the nature of the military today only further reveals the pervasiveness of the business-defined consensus, as well as the institutional levers by which the men of power apply their resources to attain their ends . . . suffice it to say the facts reinforce the point that not mythical 'military-industrial' complex but civilian authority and civilian-defined goals are the sources of American foreign and military policy—and the American malaise. . . . Moreover, it is in terms of the world economy that the business and economic backgrounds of the men of power become especially germane, for their perception of the world and United States objectives in it reflects their attempt to apply overseas the structural relations which fattened their interests at home." [21]

If one must choose between Schlesinger's and Kolko's views, one, I believe, would have to choose Kolko's. The Pentagon Papers offer, I believe, a resounding justification of this position. Max Frankel, in summing up their revelations, has this to say: "Of all the revelations in the Pentagon papers, the most important deal with the patterns of thought and action that recur at almost every stage of the U.S. involvement in Indochina. *This was a war not only decreed but closely managed by the civilian leaders of the United States.* The military chiefs were in fact reluctant at the start, unimpressed by the strategic significance of Vietnam and worried throughout that they would never be allowed to expand the size and scope of the war to the point where they could achieve a clear advantage over the enemy. This was not a war into which the United

[21] *The Roots of American Foreign Policy* (Boston: Beacon Press, 1969), pp. xii–xiv.

States stumbled blindly, step by step, on the basis of wrong intelligence or military advice that just a few more soldiers or a few more air raids would turn the tide. The nation's intelligence analysts were usually quite clear in their warnings that contemplated escalations of force and objective would probably fail. . . . The public claim that the United States was only assisting a beleaguered ally who really had to win his own battle was never more than a slogan. South Vietnam was essentially the creation of the United States. The U.S. leaders, believing that they had to fight fire with fire to ward off a communist success, hired agents, spies, generals and presidents where they could find them in Indochina. They thought and wrote of them in almost proprietary terms as instruments of U.S. policy. . . . The U.S. military and civilian bureaucracies . . . viewed themselves as being on a fixed course. They took seriously and for the most part literally the proclaimed doctrines of successive National Security Council papers that Indochina was vital to the security interests of the United States. They thus regarded themselves as obliged to concentrate always on the questions of what to do next, not whether they should be doing it." [22]

What is truly impressive is the continuity of the expansionist policy of involvement through the administrations of Truman, Eisenhower, Kennedy, Johnson, and Nixon. Such differences as exist relate to tactics and reflect the changing historical scene. But the drive and the blind commitment is always there—such a commitment indeed, that "top secret war plans during the Eisenhower administration called for the United States to destroy China if the U.S. became involved in a nuclear war with the Soviet Union." And the commitment seems to be stemming from the civilian elite of the U.S. Establishment. It is an interesting and revealing aspect of this process that it was a military man who undermined the "destroy

[22] New York Times Service, in the Toronto *Globe and Mail*, July 6, 1971.

141

China" policy. "The policy was changed . . . after objections were raised in 1961 by then–marine corps commandant David M. Shoup. Gen. Shoup, who retired in 1963, confirmed in an interview that he had objected to 'shooting in all directions' in the event of nuclear war with the Soviet Union. 'I thought it was inhuman to kill many millions of people (in China) when not only had they nothing to do with starting war, but even their government might be innocent,' he said."[23]

This unbroken thread of blind commitment exhibited by the postwar American administrations exhibits to an impressive degree the higher immorality so strikingly described by C. Wright Mills: ". . . [the] level of moral sensibility that now prevails is not merely a matter of corrupt men. The higher immorality is a systematic feature of the American elite; its general acceptance is an essential feature of the mass society. Of course, there may be corrupt men in sound institutions, but when institutions are corrupting many of the men who live and work in them are necessarily corrupted. In the corporate era, economic relations become impersonal—and the executive feels less personal responsibility. Within the corporate worlds of business, war-making and politics, the private conscience is attenuated—and the higher immorality is institutionalized. It is not merely a question of a corrupt administration in corporation, army, or state; it is a feature of the corporate rich, as a capitalist stratum, deeply intertwined with the politics of the military state."[24]

* * * * *

[23] Toronto *Daily Star*, July 6, 1971.
[24] *The Power Elite*, p. 343.

Peaceful Coexistence and Counter-Revolution

The military in the United States reflects and conforms to the values of the managerial-capitalist elite of the corporate world. Thus, the source of the counter-revolutionary dynamic of the United States today must be sought above all in the values of its managerial-capitalist elite. And these values, in turn, can be interpreted historically only in reference to the overall dynamic of the socioeconomic system of which this elite constitutes an integral part. Inevitably, therefore, the expansionist dynamic of the United States must be understood as a feature, an aspect of its socioeconomic system.

I have branded this system paternalistic capitalism, and I have examined in a limited way some aspects of its behavior. It is essential to recognize now that expansion beyond its own shores is one of the essential attributes of paternalistic capitalism. Furthermore, it is mandatory to keep in mind that this expansion is not only military, not only even jointly military and economic. *It is an expansion of the system as a whole— which tends to reproduce everywhere, wherever it reaches out on the geosphere, the structure of relations that support it at home.*

What we are concluding here, simply stated, is that paternalistic capitalism, present-day American capitalism, is imperialistic, in a sense quite different from that which was characteristic of the behavior of the empires of yesteryear. The term is intended to convey, to capture, the expansionist dynamic which springs from "the laws of motion" of the system as a whole.[25]

[25] Not surprisingly, this dynamic is absent in the Soviet Union. And this despite the growing importance of the Soviet military caste in Russia's bureaucratic establishment.

The New Mercantilism

On June 12, 1969, Gabriel Valdes, the Foreign Minister of Chile, made the following statement to President Nixon: "It is generally believed that our continent receives real financial aid. The data show the opposite. We can affirm that Latin America is making a contribution to financing the development of the United States and of the other industrialized countries. Private investment has meant and does mean for Latin America that the sums taken out of our continent are several times higher than those that are invested. Our potential capital declines. The benefits of invested capital grow and multiply enormously, though not in our countries but abroad. The so-called aid, with all its well known conditions, means markets and greater development for the developed countries, but has not in fact managed to compensate for the money that leaves Latin America in payment of the external debt and as a result of the profits generated by direct private investment. In one word, we know that Latin America gives more than it receives. On these realities, it is not possible to base any solidarity or even any stable or positive cooperation."[1]

[1] Quoted in André Gunder Frank, "The Underdevelopment Policy of the United Nations in Latin America," *NACLA Newsletter* (North American Congress on Latin America), Vol. 3, No. 8, December 1969, p. 1.

Valdes spoke the truth—and not just for Latin America. Kari Levitt, in an excellent monograph sums up the relevant evidence in a very effective manner:

"The rate of American corporate expansion by means of foreign investment did not attain its current momentum until the post–Second World War era. In 1950 the book value of the U.S. direct investment assets abroad was a mere $11 billion; by 1960 it had grown to $32 billion and in 1966 had reached $55 billion. The value of assets of U.S.-controlled manufacturing facilities abroad increased from $3.8 billion in 1950 to $22.1 billion in 1966.

"These investments are so profitable that annual remittances of dividends, royalties, license fees, rentals and management charges exceeded the value of new capital outflows in every year since 1900, with the exception of the depression years of 1928–31. The flow into the U.S. of profits and royalties during the eight-year period 1960–67 amounted to $33.3 billion—slightly more than total U.S. income from foreign direct investments over the previous sixty years ($31.7 billion). Currently remittances from U.S. subsidiaries to the metropolis are running at the level of $5.5 billion per annum, with a further $1.5 billion of non-remitted, reinvested profit. The net contribution of foreign direct investments to the U.S. balance of payments in terms of the surplus of remitted income over new capital outflows was $13.8 billion over the eight-year period 1960–67, almost as much as the net contribution of $14.5 billion over the previous sixty years.

"These 'capital-income' balances underestimate the total effect of foreign subsidiaries on the metropolitan economy. To the remitted profits and royalties must be added the increase in the book value of foreign assets by the ploughing back of retained earnings in hinterland countries, and the boost to the profitability of domestic industry by the generation of new markets for commodity exports and the availability of new raw materials on favourable terms.

"A regional breakdown reveals the fact that the 'Development Decade' of the 1960's has witnessed a substantial transfer of income from poorer to richer areas through the system of multinational corporations. In the period 1960–67, U.S. subsidiaries took $8.8 billion out of Latin America in remitted profits while investing only $1.7 billion; from the Middle East, Africa, Asia and the Far East they extracted $11.3 billion in profits while investing $3.9 billion. The funds extracted from the poorer areas of the world were, in effect transferred to the rich and growing markets of Europe, where U.S. direct investment inflows of $9.6 billion exceeded the remittance of profits of $7.3 billion." [2]

This impressive evidence seems to confirm the Neo-Marxist view. The United States stepped in the shoes of Great Britain, whose performance in the half century before the First World War—in terms of net investment overseas and return on that investment—was strikingly similar to that of the United States in the post–Second World War period. In Neo-Marxist terms, the capitalist metropolis (Britain first, then the United States) extracted "surplus" from the less developed world—especially from the least developed—to finance its own development at home and to buttress its international police force. In these terms, metropolitan development and peripheral underdevelopment are but two sides of the same coin.

But the extraction of "surplus" from the periphery (or satellite region, or hinterland) is probably the only significant similar feature in the performance of the two capitalist metropolitan centers. There are significant differences, centering around the emergence of a new instrumentality in international business—the polyglot, or multinational corporation. It is, without doubt, the most advanced, the most powerful private institution on the contemporary world scene. The structure and behavior of the multinational corporation both at

[2] *Silent Surrender* (Toronto: Macmillan of Canada, 1970), pp. 93–94.

home and abroad, its intimate relationship with the metropolitan government, especially with its military and intelligence arms, and the resulting nexus between private economic gain and the promotion of the strategic-security interests of the metropolis—all these features taken together justify the characterization of the global expansive dynamic of the emerging system as neo-mercantilist.

But what exactly is the multinational corporation? Main-line economist Neil H. Jacoby provides a clear-cut definition: "A multinational corporation owns and manages businesses in two or more countries. It is an agency of *direct,* as opposed to *portfolio,* investment in foreign countries, holding and managing physical assets rather than securities based upon these assets. . . . *Only when an enterprise confronts the problems of designing, producing, marketing, and financing its products within foreign markets does it become truly multinational.*"[3] As of the late sixties there were over two hundred U.S.-based multinational corporations, as against fewer than thirty based in other countries. Their production exceeded the $300 billion mark, an indication that a huge component of the total trade among nations has already been internalized. And the process is only in its infancy, for the rate of growth of the American multinational corporation is close to twice that of domestic corporations.

The distinctive difference between the multinational corporations and their mercantilist antecedents lies in the fact that they "have added large on-site manufacturing in foreign countries to the older activity of extracting agricultural and mineral materials for use in the home country."[4] The overall implications of this should be clear. As the corporate giant becomes polyglot and spreads its tentacles across national boundaries, it extends its control over resource allocation beyond the shores

---

[3] "The Multinational Corporation," *Center Magazine,* Vol. 3, No. 3, May 1970, p. 38. The emphasis is mine.
[4] Levitt, *Silent Surrender,* p. 31.

of the metropolis to the periphery. The paternalistic pattern of resource allocation, already established in the metropolitan center, is exported to satellite regions through the remarkable instrumentality of the multinational corporation.[5]

Since the decision horizon of the multinational corporation extends far beyond the shores of the host country, while the corporate decision center remains located in the metropolis, the allocation and development of the host country's resources is twisted to serve the values and norms of the giant corporate guest. The larger the presence of the multinational corporation in some host country, the more likely it is that the country's overall development will be made to conform to the developmental requirements of the corporate system—as these requirements are interpreted and formulated by the metropolitan Establishment. "Since the strategy of most countries stresses the expansion of the small privileged 'modern' sector rather than improving the standard of living of the bottom two-thirds, demand will shift more and more in the direction of consumer durables and brandname products including processed foods, drugs and medicines, cosmetics, fountain pens, etc., towards the mass middle class markets. . . . Since income is distributed very unevenly (in the host countries), the top 10% of the population who get anywhere from 30–40% of the total income of the country, form an important consumption group with habits roughly similar to those that prevail in the developed countries. This group is growing relatively rapidly and forms a moderately sizeable market. Every major firm in the world has to ensure that it acquires a stake in this market. . . . These underdeveloped areas are markets of the future and the

[5] We should keep in mind that nations or regions in terms of politico-economic power, form a pyramidal structure. Every nation not at the apex of a power pyramid is a satellite vis-à-vis some metropolis, while at the same time it may well be a metropolis vis-à-vis some other nation or region. Almost every Western European country has come to be a satellite vis-à-vis the United States. But this does not prevent some from being metropolitan centers vis-à-vis some Third World country or countries.

investments by large firms there are often defensive pre-emptive actions to preserve their market position."[6]

Furthermore, as the multinational corporate system continues to grow in importance on the international scene, the global pattern of resource development may well come increasingly under its command, in the context of a more or less definite global hierarchical structure. "A system of North Atlantic Multinational Corporations would tend to produce a hierarchical division of labor between geographical regions corresponding to the vertical division of labor within the firm. It would tend to centralize high-level decision-making occupations in a few key cities in the advanced countries, surrounded by a number of regional subcapitals, and confine the rest of the world to lower levels of activity and income, i.e., to the status of towns and villages in a new Imperial System. Income, status, authority, and consumption patterns would radiate out from these centers along a declining curve, and the existing pattern of inequality and dependency would be perpetuated. The pattern would be complex, but the basic relationship between different countries would be one of the superior and subordinate, head office and branch plant, between head and hand."[7]

Thus, the global development pattern that is fostered by this new mercantilism goes hand in hand with a peculiar internationalism. National barriers are bypassed or liquidated from within, while the satellitic national economics are built in the image of the metropolis—or rather, one should say, as a caricature of the metropolis. For what is propagated is a duality in the socioeconomic structure of the satellite economy. There develops an advanced sector that is drawn into the vortex of the expanding global command of the metropolitan Establishment, and a backward sector that is characterized by poverty, unemployment, and an anemic rate of growth. The importance of the

[6] Stephen Hymer, "Partners in Development," *New Statements*, Vol. 1, No. 1, 1971, p. 6.
[7] *Ibid.*, p. 8.

backward sector varies from case to case. Generally speaking, the greater the population mass of the satellite nation, and the less developed its economy, the greater is the importance of the backward sector and the more acute the evidence of poverty and unemployment in it. Thus, the development of the poorer nations of the world, in the context of this new mercantilism, is characterized by a sharp increase in the inequality of income distribution. This should come as no surprise. Since the satellites are net exporters of capital to the metropolis, the development of an adequate market for the metropolis-based multinational corporations that operate within their frontiers is dependent upon the development of a middle class that commands a significant proportion of the satellite nation's income.

There is something possibly misleading in the image, sketched in the few preceding paragraphs, of a harmonious extension of the paternalistically planned economy of the metropolis to the paternalistic-capitalist planning of the imperial periphery. The character of the game in the periphery, at this stage of its development, is basically quite different from its home-based version. It is characterized by a type of competition among the polyglot giants no longer typical of the competitive game in the metropolis: the competition among the major corporate contestants in the arena provided by the expanse of the Third World is no less than an all-out struggle for control—control over raw materials, labor supplies, product markets, financial institutions, parliaments, and governments.

The distinction is of the essence. The corporate giants compete at home within a more or less stable framework of rules.

The dominant theme at home is that of decentralized capitalist planning, which emerges as the result, jointly, of the concentration of power and the fundamentally cooperative strategies followed by the giant corporations. But in the periphery the competitive game knows no bounds, accepts no restraints. For this indeed is the era of conquest for the polyglot corporation.

Thus, in terms of the character of the competitive game among the corporate giants, we should note a polarization between its version in the metropolis and its version in the hinterland. In the metropolis the competitive game takes place within a more or less given structure, which is affected by the game in only marginal ways. The structure may evolve, but it is not shocked into major and sudden changes. In sharp contrast, in the hinterland or periphery, the competitive game occurs at a power level—a level involving discrete, substantial changes in the terms of access to raw materials, labor supplies, marketing channels and markets, credit, and tax relief.

The domestic scene of the United States in the late nineteenth century and into the twentieth was characterized by aggressive, unbridled competition among the emerging corporate giants—that is, by competition at the power level. With the advent of the Great Depression, but especially with the advent of the Second World War, the competitive pattern took on increasingly the characteristics of implicit or tacit oligopolistic cooperation which, in its mature form and against the background of an impressive degree of concentration of private economic power, provided the requisite mechanisms for decentralized, capitalist planning. Simultaneously with this "decline of competition" at home, involving mostly a change in channels and intensity, there developed intense competition for the control over the peripheral economies of the empire. And the prime vehicle, the necessary (though not sufficient) condition for effective control, is direct investment in productive facilities abroad.

In the measure that the competing multinational corporations succeed in developing a reasonably stable equilibrium in, or a generally acceptable distribution of power or control over a peripheral economy, in that measure they may be expected to extend to it the cooperative style which is characteristic of their behavior in the metropolitan center. But until that mature state of affairs is reached, one should expect the competitive game among them to be of the cut-throat variety.

Stephen Hymer predicts that "the present trend indicates further multinationalization of all giant firms, European as well as American. In the first place, European firms, partly as a reaction to the United States penetration of their markets, and partly as a natural result of their own growth, have begun to invest abroad on an expanded scale and will probably continue to do so in the future, and even to enter the United States market. This process is already well under way and may be expected to accelerate as time goes on. The reaction of United States business will most likely be to meet foreign investment at home with more foreign investment abroad. They, too, will scramble for market positions in underdeveloped countries and attempt to get an even larger share of the European market, as a reaction to European investment in the United States. Since they are large and powerful, they will on balance succeed in maintaining their relative standing in the world as a whole—as their losses in some markets are offset by gains in others. A period of rivalry will prevail until a new equilibrium between giant U.S. firms and giant European and Japanese firms is reached, based on a strategy of multinational operations and cross penetration." [8]

But is the national identity of the multinational corporations truly relevant to their behavior? Is the achievement eventually of some global equilibrium dependent exclusively on the

[8] "The Multinational Corporation and the Law of Uneven Development," in J. N. Bhagwati, ed., *Economics and World Order* (New York: World Law Fund, 1970).

behavior patterns of the multinational giants, or must it be coordinated with the achievement of an overall global balance of power among the relevant nation-states? To ask this question, is to answer it. The corporate conglomerates of today have intimate and close ties with the state apparat of their home-base. The interpenetration or overlap of the two elites, the state elite (especially that segment of it concerned with the management of national security) and the corporate elite, is such as to preclude, in the foreseeable future, a genuine internationalization of the multinational corporation. But beyond this overlap, there is also the mutual reliance of the corporation and the nation-state on the services that each can offer to a common cause. The national armies suppress insurgency and open the way for the corporate take-over of the liberated areas; while the multinational corporation integrates the periphery's economy into the empire. Thus, the relative economic power of the multinational corporation, when grouped by national origin, reflects, in general, the hierarchical structure of the nation-states that make up the capitalist world. Western Europe and Japan are junior partners in the grand capitalist alliance that is dominated by the United States. A whole range of institutions, from NATO to the International Monetary Fund, provide the "international" institutional framework which guarantees the United States the senior position in the overall economic, political, and military balance of power within the Western world. "The United States as leader has the economic power to invade the industry and markets of its chief trading partners and politico-military allies. It has the resources to maintain a dominant world military position. It can carry on foreign aid, invest in and lend to the underdeveloped countries, thus tying them closer to the United States through the resulting financial dependency of these countries. All of this, plus the maintenance of prosperity and fending off depressions, is made feasible because of the position of the United States as the world banker and of the dollar as the world reserve currency. And it can be the world banker and supply the reserve currency, because of the cooperation its military and economic strength commands among the other industrialized nations."[9]

The fact that the rivalry among the multinational giants parallels and reflects the rivalry among the political entities that make up the capitalist world has been forcefully put forth by Servan-Schreiber. "There is a crucial disproportion between investments made by Europeans in the United States, which usually comprise little more than the purchase of securities, and investments made by Americans in Europe, which often involve a real seizure of control. It is a historical rule that politically and economically powerful countries make direct investments (and gain control) in less-developed countries. Thus, European capital used to flow into Africa—not for simple investment, but to gain economic power and exploit local resources. Economically weak countries, suffering from the reverse side of the same classic law, see their savings seep away to the stronger countries in the form of investments. This is precisely what is happening today in the underdeveloped countries of Africa, where the property-owning classes invest their savings in Europe.

"There are only three possible strategies for European industry today, but we have not yet made a conscious choice among them. 1. Continue along the same path and face a double decline in our business level and our financial structure. For a time our industry could continue its struggle with American competition, but this would only delay the day of reckoning. . . . This is the strategy of retreat which leads to industrial annexation. 2. A cleverer strategy for the firm would be to try to play a complementary role in the American economy by specializing in those areas where Europe still has an advantage—largely because of lower labor costs and the use of for-

[9] Harry Magdoff, *The Age of Imperialism* (New York & London: Modern Reader, 1969), p. 109.

eign patents. While this is good strategy for a single firm, if it were applied throughout Europe it would mean splitting the world economy into three zones: a first zone of highly developed technological societies responsible for discoveries and innovations; a second zone, mainly Europe, whose role would be to produce the discoveries made elsewhere; finally, a third zone of underdeveloped nations to provide raw materials and simple industrial products using traditional methods. This division of labor is now taking place. The nations of Europe would become *industrial satellites* and could not hope to play a major role on the world stage. The more rigorous the control exercised by the dominant power, the less chance there would be for economic growth in Europe. 3. As an alternative to annexation or satellization, there is the choice of *competition*. This demands that European businesses, particularly those in the area of 'Big Science,' become fully competitive on the global market. Figures show that they cannot do this from their own resources, and that government assistance is necessary, particularly in such areas as electronics, data processing, space research, and atomic energy. How would we envisage such a massive program of government aid for the construction of giant European industries? On a national level, given the relative weakness of the individual states, such a solution would demand strict specialization. Each state would have to opt for the Swedish or Swiss example, specializing in two or three industrial areas and concentrating its resources along these lines. (The Swedish model is rich in social potential, but Sweden has no ambition to be a world power.) Only on a Europe-wide level, rather than a national one, could we hope to meet the American challenge on all major fronts. But not just any kind of European cooperative effort. . . . If we want to achieve our ambitions, make unpopular decisions, avoid duplication and waste, and draw ourselves up to a level where we can compete, we will have to give the Common Market financial power of its own. Leaving aside questions of ideology, there is no other solution to our industrial problems than forming some kind of federal organization, one whose outlines we shall try to draw as precisely as possible so that we can avoid the emotions and polemics that go with abstract ideas."[10]

Servan-Schreiber's proposal is for competition, on equal terms, of European business with American business at the level of the multinational corporation; a proposal whose feasibility depends on the willingness of the European nation-states to form a federation. Barring such a political development, the only acceptable European alternative is that of satellization. And this, of course, is exactly what is taking place today. For the United States it represents an optimal strategy. "By penetrating the metropolitan centers of Europe, U.S. capital skims off part of the cream: it benefits from (a) the enlarged consumer markets of Western Europe and (b) the opportunity to trade through channels developed by the metropolitan centers in their relations with their dependencies."[11]

So much for the reaction of the middle-range powers to the U.S. multinational corporate invasion of Europe. One should expect to find a multiple impact of that invasion in the Third World. "The relationship between multinational corporations and underdeveloped countries is somewhat like the relationship between the national corporations in the United States and state and municipal governments. These lower-level gov-

[10] J. J. Servan-Schreiber, The American Challenge (New York: Atheneum, 1969), pp. 12, 109–111.
[11] Magdoff, The Age of Imperialism, p. 16.

ernments tend always to be short on funds compared to the federal government, which can tax a corporation as a whole. Their competition to attract corporate investment eats up their surplus, and they find it difficult to finance extensive investments in human and physical capital even where such investment would be productive. This has a crucial effect on the pattern of government expenditure. What chance is there that these lower-level legislatures would approve the phenomenal expenditures on space research that now go on? A similar discrepancy can be expected in the international economy with overspending and waste by metropolitan governments and a shortage of funds in the less advanced countries. The tendency of the multinational corporations to erode the power of the nation state works in a variety of ways. . . . In general, most governmental policy instruments (monetary policy, fiscal policy, wage policy, etc.) diminish in effectiveness the more open the economy and the greater the degree of foreign investments. This tendency applies to political instruments as well as economic, for the multinational corporation is a medium by which laws, politics, foreign policy and culture of one country intrude into another. This acts to reduce the sovereignty of all nation states, but again the relationship is asymmetrical, for the flow tends to be from the parent to the subsidiary, not vice versa. The United States can apply its anti-trust laws to foreign subsidiaries to stop them from 'trading with the enemy' even though such trade is not against the laws of the country in which the branch plant is located. However, it would be illegal for an underdeveloped country which disagreed with American foreign policy to hold a U.S. firm hostage. This is because the legal rights are defined in terms of property-ownership and the various subsidiaries of a multinational corporation are not 'partners in a multinational endeavor' but the property of the general office. . . . It seems that a regime of multinational corporations would offer underdeveloped countries neither national independence nor equality. It would tend to inhibit the attainment of these goals. It would turn the underdeveloped countries into branch-plant countries, not only with reference to their economic functions but throughout the whole gamut of social, political, and cultural roles. The subsidiaries of multinational corporations are typically among the largest corporations in the country of operations, and their top executives play an influential role in the political, social and cultural life of the host country. Yet these people, whatever their title, occupy at best a medium position in the corporate structure and are restricted in authority and horizons to a lower level of decision making. The governments with which they deal tend to take on the same middle management outlook, since this is the only range of information and ideas to which they are exposed." [12]

The interventionist pattern of the multinational corporation transcends the frontiers of the economy of the host country. It reaches out to all aspects of the society of the peripheral nation, for there exists an intimate relationship between the structure of power and the developmental path of an economy. The developmental path is not, cannot be, neutral vis-à-vis the structure of power. For development necessarily affects the following dimensions: the ratio of consumption to national income; the personal distribution of wealth; the functional distribution of income; the regional distribution of economic activity; the extent to which nondomestic resources will be used and the conditions under which they will be accepted; and the role of the State in the process. Meaningful changes along these lines are bound to bring about changes in the structure of power. Thus, clearly, certain patterns of economic development in a host country would be directly hostile to the presence, operations, or success of the multinational corporation. Indeed, anything that smacks of nationalism, socialism, or

[12] Hymer, "The Multinational Corporation and the Law of Uneven Development."

meaningful social planning constitutes a clear and present danger to the multinational corporate guests. Not surprisingly, therefore, the multinational corporations, being significant partners in the Establishments of the host countries, are actively engaged behind the scenes or openly in those countries' internal political life. Inevitably, they become identified with the conservative political forces supporting the status quo. Ready though they may be to bribe the bureaucracies and buy their way into plush colonial contracts, they become the arbiters of "fiscal responsibility" and "sound monetary management." In this they are actively supported not only by metropolis-based development aid organizations (such as AID), but also by such international agencies as the IMF and the World Bank and more generally by the international business and finance community of the West. For it should be kept in mind that "fiscal irresponsibility"—almost always associated with some kind of inflationary pattern—is often the symptom of policies aimed at the redistribution of income in favor of the poorer segments of the population in a satellite nation. For the multinational corporation, any populist tendencies of this sort constitute danger signals. Thus, the metropolis-based global Establishment can rely on so-called international lending institutions to impose clear and definite limits to the policy prerogatives of satellite national governments in return for making development capital available. And this explains, of course, why development aid is *not* channeled through the United Nations.

But there is more. The symbiotic relationship at home between the managerial-capitalist elite, the national security managers, and the leadership of the military caste has its counterpart in the peripheral countries. Military alliances and Cold War blocs constitute a case in point. In Europe, for instance, what is especially relevant—beyond the economic infiltration that goes on unabated—is the revolutionary change

159

that has taken place in the role of NATO. NATO has developed into a hierarchical, international military structure, a pyramid of command that finds its apex in the Pentagon. This Pentagon-dominated military structure constitutes a network of power that has spread through the West, commanding the allegiance of satellite-national armies. And it intervenes in all aspects of the life of the participating countries, being intensely political. But quite beyond their role as the strong-arm of the metropolitan Establishment in allied nations, the armed forces of the metropolis are engaged in more or less global counter-revolutionary operations—intended to prevent, to the extent possible, the consolidation in the Third World of an "un-American Way of Life."

The new mercantilism—the global aspect of paternalistic capitalism—seems to combine Cold War strategic considerations with the expansion of the economic power of the metropolitan Establishment. Once again, but in a different fashion, the course of economic development of the poor nations is determined less by the internal growth possibilities of their economies, less by the spontaneous aspirations of the native populations, than by the growth requirements and the strategic interests of Big Brother.

The traditional Marxist analysis of imperialism lays great emphasis on the exploitation, the plunder of backward countries by the imperial powers. In my opinion this view, valid though it is, bypasses an even more important issue. The heart of the problem seems to me to lie in the fact that the growth pattern, the structure of growth of the periphery is channeled in paths which reflect the requirements of the metropolis rather than its own requirements. Furthermore, the process is cumulative. Every option for a particular use of resources at a particular time, once lost, may never appear again. The history of the peripheries is the history of cumulatively lost options.

Insurgence and revolution are the natural consequences of

this state of affairs. Gradualism does not challenge the periphery's path over time in a fundamental way. It yields to the historical necessity, accepting the loss of options as a given of the situation. Insurgency, the revolutionary approach in the Third World, reflects, in contrast, a decision for carving out for the periphery an entirely different opportunity set than is otherwise available, for extending and widening the time horizon of the economy and the society in question. Thus, revolution calls for a confrontation with the Establishment, which is metropolis-dominated. It identifies itself with national liberation. It places the political act ahead of the economic act.

Social
Planning

Socialism, having established a beachhead half a century ago, has since spread out rapidly over the globe as the major challenger, as the key practicable alternative to the capitalist mode of social organization. According to Marx's vision, it should have ushered in a classless society, free of the antagonisms, the contradictions that are characteristic not only of capitalism but of all the societies of the past. In Marx's terms: "In the social production of their lives, men enter into certain definite relationships, indispensable to them and independent of their will: these are the relationships of production, which correspond to a specific stage in the development of their material productive forces. The sum total of these relationships of production constitutes the economic structure of society, the real foundation upon which the juridical and political superstructure rises, and to which specific forms of social consciousness correspond. It is the mode of production in material life that determines the general process of men's social, political, and intellectual life. It is not men's consciousness that determines their being; on the contrary, it is their social being that determines their consciousness. At a certain stage in their development, the material productive forces of society come

162

into conflict with the existing relationships of production or —which is only a legal term for the same thing—with the property relationships within which they have hitherto been at work. These relationships become transformed from developmental forms of the productive forces into their fetters. Then begins an epoch of social revolution. With the change in the economic foundation, the whole of the giant superstructure is with greater or less rapidity also transformed. In any consideration of such transformations a distinction should always be drawn between the material transformation of the economic conditions of production, which can be defined with precision by natural science, and the juridical, political, religious, aesthetic or philosophical transformations, in short, the ideological forms in which men become conscious of the conflict and fight it out. Just as the judgment of an individual is not based on what he thinks of himself, so our judgment of such a period of transformation cannot be based on its own consciousness; on the contrary, we have to explain this consciousness from the contradictions of material life, from the conflict existing between the social productive forces and the relationships of production. No social structure ever perishes before all the productive forces for which it has room have developed; and new, higher relationships of production never appear before the material conditions for their existence have formed in the womb of the old society itself. And so mankind sets itself only the tasks it is capable of carrying out; since, on more close examination, it will always be found that the task itself arises only when the material conditions for carrying it out already exist or are at least in the process of formation. In broad outline, the Asiatic, ancient, feudal, and modern bourgeois modes of production can be designated as progressive epochs in the economic formation of society. *The bourgeois relationships of production are the last antagonistic form of the social process of production—antagonistic not in the sense of*

163

individual antagonism but in the sense of its arising out of the social living conditions of individuals; while at the same time the productive forces developing in the womb of bourgeois society create the material conditions for resolving that antagonism. Then with this social formation the prehistory of human society comes to its close." [1]

Somehow, the millennium did not arrive. The antagonisms within the society of the Soviet Union as well as those between the Soviet Union as a nation and its European satellites have been nothing short of fierce. The Stalinist period is a monument to the ruthless extermination of dissent within the Soviet bloc.

Since Stalin's death, and with the return of power to the apparat of the Communist Party, the oppressive character of the regime has progressively softened. However, this softening did not prevent the Hungarian bloodbath of 1956, nor the invasion of Czechoslovakia by the military forces of the Warsaw Pact in the summer of 1968.

The fierce antagonisms within the fabric of Soviet society are associated with both internal and external conditions. There is much truth to the Soviet apologists' argument that Soviet socialism has had to fend for its life not only against the openly hostile climate of a predominantly bourgeois world, but also against the aggressive military and economic containment policies of the United States. In the light of the demands imposed on the Soviet Union's society and economy by the confrontation with the capitalist West, it is not surprising that the Soviet State took on the dimensions of a veritable Leviathan. Nor is it surprising that the national interests of the Soviet Union took predominance over the interests of world socialism. Undoubtedly, these tendencies were reinforced by

[1] From "A Contribution to the Critique of Political Economy," in *Selected Works of K. Marx and F. Engels*, Vol. 1, pp. 337–339, as quoted in Milovan Djilas, *The Unperfect Society* (New York: Harcourt, 1969), pp. 133–135. The emphasis is mine.

the background of a Greek Orthodox and Czarist Russia; the tradition of absolutism that the Soviet Union inherited from Czarist Russia has had much to do with the manner in which it responds to the threats from abroad.

Intimately related to these developments, indeed, flowing directly out of them, was the conflict or antagonism between the tendency of the satellites to define their own national course and that of the Soviet Union, as a nation, to strengthen its control over them. This conflict between centrifugal and centripetal forces within the Soviet bloc is substantially a reflection of the global confrontation between the Soviet Union and the United States of America.

Transcending this interpretation of the sources of antagonism and conflict within the Soviet society is an interpretation that links conflict and contradictions to the transition from a capitalist to a communist society. The revolutionary transformation of society by an enlightened elite necessarily implies conflict, and this is actually anticipated in Marxist literature. Socialism is considered to be the first phase in the march toward communism, a phase during which the proletariat (actually, the Party), having assumed power, would employ it for the elimination of the remaining social and ideological strongholds of the bourgeoisie. Communism, the second and final phase, would witness the liquidation of the State as a conflict-resolving institution. Thus, the presence of conflict, and along with it of a fairly robust State, does not constitute a puzzle for the Marxists. What does constitute a puzzle for them is the emergence and consolidation of a "new class" society.

Djilas' "new class" is, in the Soviet Union, in command of a vast state machinery that plans not only the economy but almost every aspect of the society in a highly centralized fashion. The Soviet Union's Establishment consists of the top echelons of the party bureaucracy, the state bureaucracy—

165

with a prominent position reserved for the military caste—and the managerial bureaucracy. There is little doubt that the party bureaucracy is the senior partner of the coalition that defines the Soviet Establishment, corresponding in position to the managerial-capitalist elite in the Establishment of the United States. The dominant and ruling new class in the Soviet Union's highly centralized, state-controlled society merges imperceptibly into the Establishment—indeed, it *is* the Establishment. The Soviet citizen has had no effective voice over the plans or the policies adopted by the Soviet bureaucracy. Furthermore, he has had no protection from its arbitrariness. There is no a priori reason to expect that the Establishment of the Soviet Union will pursue objectives other than those which are consistent with the maintenance and extension of its power. The citizen will be served by the system, therefore, to the extent that his welfare contributes to the development of a robust base—and no more. The image of the Soviet Union is one of a hierarchical command society, a *paternalistic* society in the literal sense of the term. Its only "socialist" characteristic is the ownership of the means of production by the State.

For the Marxists, the demise of the bourgeoisie and the socialization of the productive wealth of a society are considered not only as the necessary, but also as the *sufficient* conditions for the building of a classless society. The emergence of a stable class structure in the Soviet Union and its European satellites constitutes the substance of the puzzle for the Marxian conceptual framework. But the puzzle can be solved. Its solution requires two deviations from the accepted dogma.

The first deviation is the recognition that "ownership" of productive wealth is inherently a vague concept. Ownership is coextensive with a bundle of rights and obligations: the right to exclude others from the use of whatever is owned by one, except on terms which are more or less well defined; the right

to dispose of what is owned in ways which are always circumscribed by law or custom; and the obligation not to use what
is owned in other particular ways. Ownership of the productive wealth of a society does not imply effective control over
that wealth, unless it consists of rights of disposal which, in
the particular historical context under consideration, are in
fact exercised by the owners. For instance, the shareholder in
the contemporary United States can effectively dispose of
his income-bearing certificates, but surely not of the physical
assets of the corporation whose shares he holds. He is a rentier,
a "beneficial" owner, the strategic control over productive
wealth having passed to the corporate managerial elite. Nor
does effective control over the productive wealth of a society
imply ownership. The managerial elite's control over the productive wealth of the United States has, in fact, little to do
with its ownership claims on that wealth. The rentier's membership in the dominant, ruling class in the United States is
guaranteed primarily not by the legal order but by his successful penetration of and assumption directly and indirectly of a
commanding position in the Establishment—in the coalition
that effectively controls the vital social, economic, and political
processes in the United States. In a society where the state
apparat effectively controls the total of its productive wealth,
those in control of the state apparat constitute the Establishment, an Establishment which in such a case is indistinguishable from the dominant, ruling class. And since in the Soviet
Union and its European satellites the bureaucracies—especially
the party bureaucracy—effectively control the State, they necessarily constitute the Establishment, as well as the dominant,
ruling class of those societies.

The second deviation is somewhat more damaging to the
Marxian conceptual framework. It is assumed in this framework that there is a one-to-one relationship between the modes
of production (technology-resources) prevalent in a society

and the emerging social relations in production—that is, the emerging class structure. But this does not seem to be valid. One negative example would be sufficient for the refutation of this proposition. And it exists. Are we prepared to argue that the Soviet Union's type of socialism was (is) the only possible one, under the modes of production that were (are) prevalent in that country? I think not. Mao's experiment in China, especially since the Cultural Revolution, constitutes living proof of the possibility of shaping social relations in production (the class structure) in alternative ways. The main target of the Cultural Revolution was the reversal of the process of centralization in planning and the attendant development of a new class society. According to Jack Gray, "It is perhaps in the idea of 'destruction of the three great differences'—among industry and agriculture, town and country, and mental and menial labor—that Mao's point of view on social and economic change is best summed up. In Karl Marx's own writings, the elimination of the social gulfs was expected to follow the creation of communism: it was a characteristic of the final classless Utopia. In Mao's thought, their elimination becomes instead the most critical step toward successful economic development in his own underdeveloped country, a step now planned in detail." [2]

Not surprisingly, Mao has been condemned by the Soviet Union's leadership as a voluntarist, as an "anti-Marxist who believes that the human will, by some magic, can wish away objective facts." [3] But the voluntarist viewpoint seems to make sense indeed in the context of a revolutionary movement that consciously attempts to shape social relations anew. And, though the objective historical conditions undoubtedly circumscribe the set of possibilities, clearly this set does not

[2] "The Economics of Maoism," in China, After the Cultural Revolution: A Selection from the Bulletin of the Atomic Scientist (New York: Vintage Books, 1970), p. 142.
[3] Ibid., pp. 115–116.

consist of just one element, or just one possibility. There remains the more fundamental problem, of course, of whether it is in principle possible that a revolutionary elite, such as the Communist Party, will proceed to shape social relations in production (the class structure) in such a way as to make way for its own demise as an elite. In a sense, this is the substance of the Maoist experiment.

Be that as it may, the Soviet Union's paternalistic socialism and planning are hardly models for imitation, hardly a genuine alternative to paternalistic and neo-mercantilist capitalism. Hierarchical Soviet planning is clearly both elitist and arbitrary. And Soviet socialism, while freeing man from the irrationality and injustice of the so-called free enterprise system, has subjected him to a new and tenacious servitude that is prized only by those privileged few that have access to the mystique of the Communist Party.

*ON PLANNING

The term planning is used in so many contexts as to convey by itself not much more than the notion of conscious or rational temporal behavior. In what immediately follows I wish to make a distinction among three types of planning in order to sharpen the concept: the first type of planning may be called societal management; the second type is development planning; and the third type is organizational design. Actually, the distinction is not hard and fast, for societal management may be made to converge to development planning, as development planning may be made to converge to organizational design.

Before examining the nature of the differences among these three types of planning, we should examine what they have in common, by reference to an abstract hypothetical situation. Assume that for the nation or the society under consideration there exists a planning authority whose task may be described as follows: The authority must select and implement one among the possible or feasible trajectories or scenarios of the society in question, and do so on the basis of an explicit ranking of alternatives that incorporates or reflects its value system. For the purposes of this discussion it is quite irrelevant whether or not the planning authority's value system is representative of the values of society at large.

A trajectory is a time path or a temporal sequence. Obviously, the concept of a societal trajectory is of staggering complexity. At every point in time it must convey all the information about the society in question that is relevant to the planning authority's task of selection and implementation. Thus, necessarily it is a multidimensional object. As an example, consider the trajectory of a missile, which may be defined by the temporal sequence of the coordinates of the physical space it traverses. Clearly, even the most elementary definition of *social space* would require a relatively large number of coordinates.[4]

Our next problem is to elucidate the concept of feasibility of a societal trajectory. Undeniably, what is or is not feasible depends on the historically given initial conditions. These initial conditions include not only the structure of the physical environment and the known technologies, but also the structure of the society in question and, indeed, its juridical, political, and cultural super-structure. All this is given objectively, and constitutes an aspect of what may be called historical necessity. Side by side with these objectively given initial conditions, there is injected a subjective element, which may be identified as the system of beliefs of the planning authority. This system of beliefs is incorporated into the theory or model of the social process held by the planning authority.

---

[4] In economic macroplanning, for instance, the "coordinates" typically include national product, consumption, investment, employment, the price level, government expenditures, government revenues, and so on.

The planning authority's model reflects its own perception of the dynamics of the social system which it is empowered to steer into the future. The construction of a theory or the selection of a model by the planning authority is a creative task and, furthermore, one subject to the limitations imposed upon the authority's field of vision by the prevailing ideology as well as by the state of social science. Be that as it may, what is or is not perceived as being feasible is necessarily subjective. Thus, the feasibility of a societal trajectory is always presumptive. Historical necessity reappears here, but in a subjective sense; that is, it is historical necessity as *perceived* by the planning authority.

The model of the social process selected by the planning authority conveys important information. It generates all the (perceived) alternative feasible temporal sequences open to the society in question once the historically given initial conditions are plugged in. Furthermore, the model specifies the instruments or levers at the disposal of the planning authority for setting the society on alternative courses or trajectories.

Naturally, if the planning authority's model is to be at all useful, it should be cast in probabilistic terms or in other terms that permit taking account of uncertainty. Thus, the planner's problem, in a realistic context, does not consist of selecting one societal trajectory but, rather, of steering society onto some subset of the totality of alternative feasible temporal sequences.

In a sense, all types of national or societal planning share the features just reviewed, since these features merely spell out the meaning of conscious or rational behavior on a national or societal scale. And now to the differences among the three types of planning.

Planning of the first type, societal management, takes as given and, to all intents and purposes, as unchangeable, the extant social structure. And this is directly manifested in the types of instruments made available (or recognized as being available) to the planning authority. In the West, characteristically, the key instruments incorporated in the governmental planning models include the rate of interest (or the supply of money), public revenues (tax rates, tariffs, etc.), and public expenditures. In the post revolutionary socialist regimes, such as the contemporary Soviet Union, the instruments are both more varied and more direct, but they, too, take the basic social structure as given and unchangeable. This type of planning is intrastructural—leaving well enough alone.

The inclusion in the planning model, on a more or less significant scale, of instruments or levers which affect social structure opens new vistas for society, vistas that are manifested in the expansion of the set of alternative feasible temporal sequences or trajectories open to that society. This is exactly what is meant by development planning. It is characteristic of all the developing countries of the Third World, and of postrevolutionary socialist regimes that have not accepted the status quo as a final state of affairs.

In truly revolutionary situations, the set of structural instruments is extended to encompass society at large, the whole fabric of societal organization. One may properly think of this third type of planning as organizational design. Organizational design constitutes social engineering on a grand scale, asserting that "natura facit saltum." Contemporary China constitutes an example of this type of planning. But the term *revolutionary* should not be interpreted as necessarily implying violent confrontations. It is applicable whenever the Establishment undergoes radical change with the displacement of the insiders by some outsiders with a new vision of society. Thus, Allende's Chile, for instance, may conceivably also fall in this category, notwithstanding the fact that the transformation seems to be taking place within the constitutional framework of that country.

Development planning and organizational design represent explicit schemes for reform-oriented social action. Of course, there arises a fundamental question: Since no theory of social change is available, since the most we can hope for as social scientists is the construction of models dealing with limited aspects of this process, how is it possible to talk about *planned* change, about social action on a global scale which is intended to produce development toward ambitious preset targets? In other words, what are the scientific foundations of development planning or organizational design? The answer, no matter how unsatisfactory, is relatively simple. Development planning or organizational design constitute particular forms of decision-making on the basis of limited information. They are no different in this respect from most forms of human action. Action and knowledge are intimately related. The processes of development planning and organizational design must be viewed as special cases of a learning process on a societal scale. This view of social theory—namely, the view that social theory emerges from an interplay of knowledge and action—implies, first, the progressive obsolescence of theory in terms of the changing problems of changing generations and in terms of the institutions which reflect the changing values of successive generations, and second, the need of a continuous reformulation of theory.

It is now time that we examine what is implied by the artifact of the planning authority that I imposed on my argument. To begin with, a planning authority is relevant only to situations where indeed there is society-wide planning—that is to say, in situations where either private or public decision centers or a mixture of both have *jointly* the intention and the power to steer society onto a path which is consistent with their preferences. In this sense, clearly a market capitalist society is *not* planned. Equally clearly, the society of the Soviet Union *is* planned. And I have argued in this book that contemporary paternalistic capitalism is converging to the status of a planned society.

But it would be an error to assume that in all instances of planned societies there exists an identifiable social instrumentality labeled the planning authority. Actually, the relevant instrumentalities, power foci, or vested interests can be multiple. In such instances of multiple decision centers, the requirements for considering society as being planned are two: First, there must exist a more or less institutionalized, explicit bargaining process among the decision centers, capable of producing a consistent preference system for the ranking of social alternatives. Second, the decision centers must be both motivated and vested with the power to steer society onto a preferred path by observing and responding to a sequence of plan-implementing signals.

Conceptually, the simplest case to visualize is that of *monocentric* planning. Monocentric planning, the case of a single decision center, of an effective central planning board, is identified with totally centralized command, and usually with totally centralized information processing. Such is the case when a central planning board selects a detailed quantitative plan and implements it by assigning quantitative targets to the behavior units (firms and consumers). Actually, it is quite possible, in principle, for the central planning board to implement some plans by issuing the proper (planning) price signals to the behavior units (firms and consumers), provided they are motivated to make all relevant decisions, in response to these price signals, according to generally accepted or previously laid down rules. Thus what is truly characteristic of monocentric planning is the total centralization of command. Information processes may be decentralized, in principle, even in this extreme case of command centralization. Monocentric planning is possibly a useful abstraction, but of little relevance to historical situations. For it represents the limiting case of *hierarchical* planning—

where there exists a clear-cut vertical command structure with an identifiable apex, but where also, at each level of decision-making, the centers are free to make choices from a meaningful set of alternatives, a set specified by the immediately superior level of command. Varying degrees of decentralization of command and of information processing are consistent with this type of planning. Far more interesting is, finally, the case of *polycentric* planning. It is similar in all respects but one to hierarchical planning. The key differentiating characteristic of polycentric planning derives from the fact that the command structure does *not* extend all the way to an apex. Somewhere along the line it is replaced by institutionalized bargaining processes among the decision-making units (be they functionally or regionally defined, or both). Naturally, these bargaining processes must be capable in principle of producing an overall, consistent society-wide preference system for the ranking of alternatives, and capable, too, of leading to the choice of some preferred path (or set of paths). Furthermore, it is essential that the decision-centers be both motivated and vested with the power to steer society onto the selected path (or set of paths). Clearly, high degrees of decentralization, both in command and in information processing, are consistent in principle with this type of planning.[5]

* "WHO, WHOM?"

I have argued or implied in this book that the choice of society today is not between planning and no planning. Given modern technology, and the quest for a rational order where man will control rather than be at the mercy of his social environment, the choice is only among kinds of planned so-

[5] The argument on pages 80–89 may now be cast in the following form: Planning in modern paternalistic capitalism is polycentric. Furthermore, given the growing internal contradictions of the system, it should be expected to converge to hierarchical planning, with a mixture of private and privately controlled public instrumentation at the apex of the pyramid of command.

cieties. By "kinds" of planned societies I am not referring to the extent of the ambitiousness characteristic of the planning process—whether it is oriented to merely managing society or to encompassing the total transformation of society. I am referring to the fundamental problem that is contained in Lenin's two-word question, "Who, Whom?"—that is, Who should decide for whom?

Of course, one could fall back on a superficial cliché and argue that in a democratic society, founded on the principle of proper and orderly representation of the interests of the citizenry in the decision-making centers through their elected representatives, the sovereignty of the people would be guaranteed—even in the case of a centralized, planned society. The corollary would seem to be that as long as the planners are accountable to the people through the instrumentalities of representative democracy, their plans will reflect the values and aspirations of the people.

But I have already argued, in discussing paternalistic capitalism, that popular sovereignty, as exercised in the modern, industrially advanced society, has but a wisp of its intended meaning. Elections have become a formality—a necessary ritual for the legitimation of a state which, while acting in the name of the people, is in fact inexorably committed to serving the interests of the Establishment and the dominant class. And what is true of paternalistic capitalism, in this respect, is of course no less true of paternalistic socialism.

Actually, the concept of democracy is a complex, synthetic concept. Two quite distinct notions, popular sovereignty and personal liberty, seem to vie for recognition under the same label. Logically, the two are unrelated. The Bill of Rights is a legislative monument to the concept of personal liberty, whereas Lincoln's "government of the people, by the people, for the people" sums up the case for popular sovereignty. So it should not be surprising to discover that Edmund Burke condemned popular sovereignty in the name of personal liberty: "No experience has taught us, that in any other cause or method than that of an hereditary crown, our liberties can be regularly perpetuated and preserved sacred as our hereditary right." Burke's king did not exercise arbitrary power. He was constrained both by custom and by Divine Law, whereas the revolutionary assembly in France, "since the destruction of the orders, has no functional law, no strict convention, no respected usage to restrain it. Instead of finding themselves obliged to conform to a fixed constitution, they have a power to make a constitution which shall conform to their designs." For "if civil society be the offspring of *convention* that convention must be its law. That convention must limit and modify all the descriptions of constitution which are formed under it." [6]

It is clear that Burke, like many of his contemporaries, thought of sovereignty as limited by convention in the context of a nominalist concept of society—and thus as capable of providing guarantees for personal liberty. In the sweep of the French Revolution, the concept of popular sovereignty, having taken the place of divine sovereignty, merged with the concept of the nation and national sovereignty. In this new context, the legitimacy of the State's commands derives from the fact that the State is the mandatory of the nation; and the beneficence of the State derives from its service to the aims of the nation. This radically new perspective is essentially organicist, expressing an image of society as a purposive, willful whole rather than as an assemblage of individuals.

Two quite distinct questions emerge: First, will the mandatory of the sovereign people—be it the executive or the legislative branch of the government—deriving, as it does, "of the people and by the people" *also* act "for the people"? What

[6] *Reflections on the Revolution in France* (New York: Dolphin Books, Doubleday, 1961), pp. 36, 57, 72.

are the guarantees? Second, what is the fate of the minority, the fate of dissent in the context of popular sovereignty? Certainly, if the rules of the game are to be fixed by a majority and in the interests of the majority, there can be no protection, in principle, for the minority. The concept of popular sovereignty, of rule "of the people, by the people, and for the people" makes no provisions for the fate of the minority. Admittedly, the Bill of Rights does so, but in the context of popular sovereignty, what are the guarantees that the Bill too will not be swept away in the majority's interest?

It is clear that the concept of democracy, as we understand it, should make provisions both for effective popular sovereignty and for meaningful personal liberty. It would seem that the necessary and sufficient conditions for a democratic process in the context of representative democracy are as follows:

1. A set of rules that make it possible for the majority to govern, that is, to make decisions in the name of the whole.

2. A set of rules that permit the members of the society—in whose name the governing body acts—to exercise continuous, informed control over it.

3. A set of rules that permit the minority to become a majority under terms that are equal to all.

4. A set of rules that specify the limits on unfavorable effects of actions on the part of the governing body on any component of the society in question.

5. A set of rules that specify the limits on unfavorable effects of action undertaken by any group or persons on any other group or person in the society in question.

The first three sets of rules encompass the concept of popular sovereignty. The remaining two define the concept of liberty. This much can be said on purely logical, definitional grounds. On historical grounds, we are bound to recognize that the enactment of such a set of demanding rules presupposes a rather unusual distribution of power. For no rules will be enacted, or observed even if enacted, unless they correspond to the prevailing structure of power.

In the modern mass society the structure of power is such that representative democracy, though providing legitimacy for the actions of the State, has become a cloak for the almost unfettered exercise of power by the Establishment.

Thus, to make planning responsive to the will and the aspirations of the common man, to turn it into genuine *social* planning, it is necessary to redistribute power—indeed, to *decentralize* it. And this decentralization, both logically and historically, can hardly be sought along functional lines. It almost inevitably must be sought along regional lines.

Even a balanced representation of all the occupational-functional groups in the bargaining process *at the top*, through which the national or social plan emerges, does not guarantee that the plan will be responsive to the aspirations of the citizens at large. For in a mass society, the leadership of a functional group on a national scale is or becomes, almost inevitably, itself a component of the Establishment and constitutes, therefore, a decision instrumentality beyond the reach of the citizen.

We speculate, therefore, that the quest for a decentralized planning structure must be built around a regional confederation. But what is a regional unit in this sense? For a possible definition I turn to a regional planner.

"To be defined, a planning region, like any form of anthropogeographic region, needs a central theme and a generating idea. In order to define an anthropogeographic framework appropriate for meaningful planning it becomes necessary to conjecture some social aims avoiding as much as possible personal opinion and fancy.

"Three basic aims are proposed.

"The first aim: *land conservation and orderly development*

of the natural resources. It points to an ecologically balanced world where man shall take his natural place next to the other organisms, animate and inanimate, which inhabit his habitat. Man shall cease depleting the natural wealth and at the same time shall free himself from the agony of hunger, and artificiality in his way of life.

"The second aim: *integration of all production forms including industry and agriculture.* Implicit here is the integration of all forms of human work, of mental with manual, of indoors with outdoors.

"The third aim: *decentralization.* This points to a world depending for its existence less on wheels and population uprootings and more on the harmonious relationship between man and his environment social and natural.

"The above aims determine five criteria for the delineation of the planning region.

"First criterion: *the region must be a geographic unit.* In other words, it must be a complete ecosystem, or a natural-biotic system.

"Second criterion: *the region must be endowed with balanced natural resources analogous to its present or potential future population.* The region should produce sufficient surplus of goods and services in exchange for what it cannot produce locally and must import from other regions. However, the region, even at a minimal standard of living, should have the potential of self-sufficiency. This is imperative to the attainment of some degree of internal security and political independence even within a larger national entity.

"Third criterion: *the region must have social cohesion.* This criterion is especially important in delineating planning regions in a long-settled country, where social groups are closely knit and attached to their environment.

"Fourth criterion: *the region must be a potential political entity not only within its present national framework but also vis-à-vis the rest of the world.* This criterion implies a certain size (area and population), and a certain potential of power, economic and political.

"Fifth criterion: *the region must be potentially efficient in terms of social and technical services and of administration.* These are the services that exert an important impact on contemporary life. Examples of such services are power and transportation networks, and water distribution networks for irrigation, industry, and urban use.

"The new region as defined above could be termed a unit-state. It is within a given setting of conditions, physical, social, technical, the smallest viable anthropogeographic entity; viable in respect to the requirements of the contemporary world.

"In the present world framework, at best approximation, it can be an integral part of a nation.

"Technical or economic considerations are not the strongest factors in delineating the new regions. In the trilogy, people, environment, techniques, the first two facts outweigh the third. Furthermore, the people will always be, or should be, the determinants of technics; how much technics and of what kind." [7]

The national entity may thus be conceived as a confederation of regional units. And the national plan emerges, therefore, as a composite of the regional plans, through an interregional bargaining process. This process is oriented to the resolution of conflicts among the regions as they arise from possible unfavorable impacts, on one or more regions, of each regional unit's planned action (or inaction); and also to the resolution of conflicts arising from unfavorable impacts on one or more regions of nationwide action (or inaction). This bargaining process is subject, of course, to rules accepted and observed by the participating regional units—for otherwise there would be no sense in talking about national planning.

[7] Antonis Tritsis, "The Nature of Planning Regions" (unpublished ms.).

Thus, interregional or national consensus is a necessary condition for the viability of the scheme.

The degree of intraregional centralization in planning—whether in terms of the structure of information or the structure of command—cannot be spelled out in abstract, generally applicable terms. Clearly, the regional decentralization scheme can be extended within the region to subregions. But then it should be expected that the scope of centralized decision-making at the regional level, vis-à-vis the subregions, will be much larger than that at the *national* level, vis-à-vis the regions. For the regional units will have been constructed, presumably, with an eye to the internalization within the region of most of the relevant externalities (external economies and diseconomies) so that due account of them may be taken in intraregional planning.

Does such a scheme guarantee the evanescence of the Establishment? Not necessarily. It may merely change its form. The key to the formation of an Establishment is the limitation to entry, the propagation of functionally distinct, noncompeting groups through privilege, be it hereditary, economic, or elitist. Thus, if we wish to exclude the possibility of the development of a new form of Establishment, we must guarantee the freedom of entry into occupations. *And this in the end requires a direct attack on specialization, and the consequent identification of an individual over his life-cycle with a function, a position, and a certain distinctive level of income and wealth.* This is undoubtedly what is meant by Tritsis' call for "the integration of all forms of human work, of mental with manual, of indoors with outdoors." For the successive assumption by each and every individual of alternative, distinct roles in the social structure undermines or eliminates the polarity that is a condition for the domination of one group by another. Furthermore, with the implied politicization of the individual, the concepts of popular sovereignty and personal liberty tend to become unified in what may well be called participatory democracy, because the national, regional, and subregional authorities, in the context of this vision, are or become "of the people, by the people, and for the people" in a *direct* rather than a representative sense.

The argument could, indeed it should, be extended to global society. The nation, after all, need not be a rationally circumscribed super-region, a rational subdivision of global human society. But a nation-free world—in terms of which the present polarized, hierarchical, oppressive, and wasteful international structure seems so irrational—cannot come about unless the structure of international power has been redressed in favor of the weaker nations, unless the satellite, peripheral nations can throw off the shackles imposed upon them by the dynamics of imperialism, super-power confrontation, and counter-revolution. Seen in this light, the proliferation of independent, sovereign national units, and the creation of new poles of power, shows up as a necessary and positive step in the process of limiting, circumscribing the power of global establishments and their imperial substructure. For the attrition of global establishments is a necessary condition for the attrition, and the eventual evanescence, of establishments at the national level.

Of course, this is just a *vision*. Its importance derives from the fact that it spells out the magnitude of the difficulties which are to be encountered in any organizational design intended to lay the foundations for *social planning*—for man's conscious, rational control over his social environment.

Index

Index

Index

Nagasaki, 126
National Liberation Front (EAM),
125
National Security Council, 141
National security managers, 7, 115,
116, 117
Neoclassical model, 9
New Deal, 9, 112
Nixon, President Richard M., 141,
144
North Atlantic Treaty Organization
(NATO), 131, 134, 135, 153,
160

Oligopolist, 50, 51, 55, 57, 58, 79
Oligopolistic market, 51, 53, 54, 56,
68, 85
Oligopoly: 55; behavior in, 51, 52;
cooperation in, 151; economy of,
79; industry in, 54, 55; strategy of,
51, 52
Organizational design, 172, 173

Palme, Olof, 20, 21
Papandreou, A. G., 95
Pareto, Vilfredo, 17
Pareto-optimality, 17
Paternalistic: defined, 6, 78, 166
Paternalistic capitalism, 6, 7, 8, 24,
79, 80, 87, 90, 91, 143, 169, 174,
175, 176
Paternalistic planning, 80, 87
Paternalistic socialism, 8, 162–168,
169
Pax Americana, 137
Peaceful coexistence, 121, 122, 123,
127, 132
Pentagon, 93, 94, 115, 133, 160
Pentagon Papers, 120, 140
Periphery (hinterland), 146, 147,
150, 160, 161
Phillips, J. D., 42
Planning: authority, 170, 171, 173,
174; capitalist, 86, 89, 151; decentralized, 6, 85, 86, 89, 151; development, 169, 172, 173; hierarchical,
169, 174, 175; monocentric, 174;
as organizational design, 169, 172,
173; paternalistic, 80, 87; polycentric, 87, 175; regional, 179, 180,
181; social, 6, 159, 183; as societal
management, 169, 171
Poland, 130

Popular Liberation Army (ELAS),
125
Potsdam Conference, 126; Agree-
ments of, 131
Price leader, 53, 85
Price leadership, 53, 54
PROMETHEUS (plan), 133
Public goods, 31, 32

Red army, 129
Rentier, 167
Roosevelt, President Franklin D., 121,
125
Rostow, W. W., 130
Ruling class, 7, 104, 105, 106, 109,
110, 167
Rumania, 124, 125, 126

Schlesinger, Arthur, Jr., 138, 140
Schuman, F. L., 131
Schumpeter, Joseph, 35, 38
Servan-Schreiber, J.-J., 154, 156
Shoup, General David M., 117,
142
Smalter, Donald J., 81
Social cost, 43, 45, 59, 60
Social waste, 45, 46
Soviet bloc, 164
Soviet socialism, 164, 169
Soviet Union, 7, 121, 122, 123, 124,
127, 129, 130, 132, 133, 135, 136,
141, 142, 164, 165, 166, 168, 169,
172, 173
Stalin, 124, 125, 126, 128, 129, 136,
137, 164
State: contrasted with Government,
97; meanings of, 95
State Department, 115
Stavrianos, L. S., 125, 126
Steiner, Peter, 34, 35
Stevenson, Adlai, 123
Surplus, 41, 42, 43, 44, 45, 46, 57,
58, 59, 60, 61, 62, 63, 87, 146
Surplus value, 42, 60
Sweden, 20, 21
Sweezy, Paul, 5, 41, 42, 43, 46, 47,
48, 50, 54, 55, 56, 58, 59, 60, 61,
80

Taylor, F. M., 25
Technostructure, 6, 64, 70, 71, 73,
74, 78, 91
Tito, Marshal, 126

Tritsis, Antonis, 181, 182
Truman, President Harry S., 127, 128, 141
Truman Doctrine, 128, 129, 131, 136
Turkey, 128

United Nations, 123, 130, 159
United States of America, 7, 63, 93, 99, 108, 110, 111, 112, 121, 122, 123, 124, 125, 127, 128, 129, 131, 132, 133, 134, 136, 138, 139, 140, 141, 143, 144, 145, 146, 148, 152, 153, 154, 159, 164, 165

USSR, *see* Soviet Union

Valdes, Gabriel, 144, 145
Vietnam, 121, 138, 140, 141

Wallace, Henry, 127
Warsaw Pact, 131, 133, 134, 135, 164
Workable competition, 24, 52, 55
World Bank, 159

Yalta, 125
Yalta Declaration, 124
Yugoslavia, 125, 128, 130